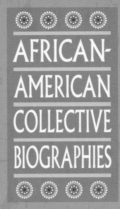

AFRICAN-
AMERICAN
COLLECTIVE
BIOGRAPHIES

Extraordinary African-American Poets

Therese Neis

Enslow Publishers, Inc.
40 Industrial Road
Box 398
Berkeley Heights, NJ 07922
USA

http://www.enslow.com

Library of Congress Cataloging-in-Publication Data

Neis, Therese.
  Extraordinary African-American poets / Therese Neis.
    p. cm. — (African-American collective biographies)
  Summary: "Read about Phillis Wheatley, Paul Lawrence Dunbar, Langston Hughes, Gwendolyn Brooks, Amiri Baraka, Jay Wright, Nikki Giovanni, Rita Dove"—Provided by publisher.
  Includes bibliographical references and index.
  ISBN 978-1-59845-139-9
  1. African American poets—Biography—Juvenile literature. 2. Poets, American—Biography—Juvenile literature. I. Title.
  PS153.N5N45 2012
  811.009′896073—dc23

                        2011019954

Future editions
Paperback ISBN 978-1-4644-0038-4
ePUB ISBN 978-1-4645-0945-2
PDF ISBN 978-1-4646-0945-9

Printed in the United States of America

032012 Lake Book Manufacturing, Inc., Melrose Park, IL

10 9 8 7 6 5 4 3 2 1

To Our Readers: We have done our best to make sure all Internet addresses in this book were active and appropriate when we went to press. However, the author and the publisher have no control over and assume no liability for the material available on those Internet sites or on other Web sites they may link to. Any comments or suggestions can be sent by e-mail to comments@enslow.com or to the address on the back cover.

Enslow Publishers, Inc., is committed to printing our books on recycled paper. The paper in every book contains 10% to 30% post-consumer waste (PCW). The cover board on the outside of each book contains 100% PCW. Our goal is to do our part to help young people and the environment too!

Poetry permissions can be found on page 109.

Illustration Credits: ©Antydiluvian, p. 15; Associated Press, pp. 40, 48, 54, 70, 74, 87; AP Images: Andrew Shurtleff, p. 83, Linda Spillers, p. 44; Library of Congress, pp. 5, 8, 10, 20, 23, 28, 32; © Photographs by Diane Krajenski, p. 60, 66; © Seattle Arts & Lectures, photo by Sheila Addleman.

Cover Illustration: Associated Press

Contents

Introduction

Writing poetry can be lonely work. Poets often sit by themselves in quiet rooms with only pens and paper for company. They struggle to find just the right words to express their most private thoughts. But the poems they write take on much broader meanings when other people read them.

For more than two centuries, African-American poets have written about their struggles to find an equal place in society. They have written of their pride and of their frustration with a society that often rejects them. Their poems explore many basic questions: Who am I: African, American, or both? How can I fit in? Do I want to? Do I want society to know my true feelings? Why and how do I matter? How can I help make the world a better place for all?

According to Michael S. Harper and Anthony Walden, editors of *The Vintage Book of African-American Poetry*, "This quest for identity and a belonging that will not compromise itself is the theme, if there can be said to be one theme" that runs throughout the history of African-American poetry.[1]

The first two African Americans to publish books of poetry were slaves.

Phillis Wheatley lived in Boston during the Revolutionary War period. Her owners were kind. They taught her to read. They raised her alongside their own daughters. Many open-minded readers in New England enjoyed her poems.[2]

George Moses Horton, on the other hand, lived in North Carolina during the Civil War era. He taught himself to read. He wrote love poems for students at Chapel Hill. His owner let him keep the money he made selling these poems. Horton tried, unsuccessfully, to buy

Hundreds of African captives were loaded onto each slave ship and forced to sit or lie side by side with no room to move and little space to breathe.

his freedom by selling copies of his first book of poems, *The Hope of Liberty*. He remained a slave until 1865. Following the ratification of the Thirteenth Amendment ending slavery, Horton was helped by General Will H. S. Banks of the Ninth Michigan Cavalry, who persuaded the William B. Smith Publishing Company of Raleigh to print a second book of Horton's poetry.[3]

Both poets lived at a time when most African Americans were legally prohibited from learning to read. The few northern slaves who could read usually weren't allowed to spend their time writing poetry. Many white readers didn't believe that African Americans were smart enough to write literature.[4] Phillis Wheatley and George Moses Horton had to prove to these doubters that African Americans were intelligent and could create true works of art.

After the Civil War, African Americans were no longer enslaved. But they did not have as much freedom as whites. Many learned to read and write, but they still faced huge problems. Their hopes for full freedom were crushed by Jim Crow laws.[5] Two famous poets active at the turn of the nineteenth century were Paul Laurence Dunbar and James Weldon Johnson. Both wrote of their struggles to find a place in the world. But they also wrote about the dashed hopes of former slaves.

A major turning point for African-American poets came during the period called the Harlem Renaissance. This artistic movement took place between the 1920s and 1930s. It was centered in the Harlem neighborhood of New York City (with offshoots in Chicago and Washington, D.C.). Members of this movement created enduring masterworks of African-American art, literature, and music. Poets from this era were proud of their African heritage. This pride inspired them to write very personally. It also moved them to demand justice for all people. During this period, white publishers began to print volumes of African-American literature.

Introduction

Langston Hughes was the best-known poet of this generation. He made the world aware of the joys and disappointments of African-American life.[6] Countee Cullen, Claude McKay, and Sterling A. Brown were other important poets of this time. Brown was famous for his 1933 book *Southern Road*. He also taught African-American literature for forty years at Howard University. He inspired countless students to become writers.[7]

Gwendolyn Brooks started writing after the Harlem Renaissance, but was influenced by its ideas. She told the stories of poor African Americans in her elegant poems. In 1950, she became the first African American to win a Pulitzer Prize.

Life has changed dramatically for African Americans since World War II. They finally began to win true freedom during the civil rights movement of the 1950s and 1960s. But they continue to face racism and prejudice in their daily lives.

Many African-American poets have become famous during the past fifty years. Yet they take such different approaches to writing that it is hard to put them into any single category. Some write about finding acceptance. Others write about the conflicts they still face. Poets such as Jay Wright continue to write in traditional American styles. Others, such as Amiri Baraka, are radical. Baraka sought to link his poetry to jazz forms, while making the civil rights movement the subject of much of his poetry.[8] He is the founder of the black arts movement.

Today, African-American writers have earned a new acceptance. In 1993, three women of color received top writing awards. Rita Dove was named Poet Laureate of the United States.[9] Toni Morrison was awarded the

Captive Africans were chained together and marched to the coast to be sent in slave ships to America.

8

Nobel Prize for Literature. President Bill Clinton invited Maya Angelou to read at his inauguration. African-American writers won more major literary awards between 1987 and 1997 than they had in the entire preceding century.[10] More recently, Elizabeth Alexander was the official poet celebrating the inauguration of President Barack Obama in 2009.

Meanwhile, African-American language, including its slang, has become a component of speech for the larger community. Popular songwriters brought the language of the street to all types of American homes. Popular poets have followed suit. Nikki Giovanni uses inner-city phrases and realistic images to create poems that reflect African-American life. By doing so, she has brought poetry to the people.

African-American poetry has come a long way. Once, leading intellectuals debated whether the "Negro was even capable" of creating meaningful works of art.[11] Now, African-American poetry has become an important part of our national culture.

A Note for Beginning Poetry Readers

Poetry often looks hard to read at first glance. The line breaks, stanzas, and odd phrases can seem confusing. The best way to understand poetry is to hear it read out loud. Try doing this yourself, or ask someone else to read a poem aloud to you.

Do not automatically stop at the line endings or stanza breaks. Often a phrase will be spread out over two lines, or two stanzas. Instead, follow the punctuation marks, even if that means stopping in the middle of one line and making no stop at the end of another.

If you are reading a modern "free-verse" poem with little punctuation, look at the capital letters. Sometimes a writer will start a new idea with a capital letter, even if there is no period before it.

Read the poem out loud once or twice to understand the meaning of the words. Then go back and read the lines again. Notice how the writer used rhyme, rhythm, or other poetic devices to create a work of literary art.

If you like the short samples of poems found in this book, try to find copies of the complete poems. Some good poetry collections are listed in the back of this book.

This illustration is the frontispiece for *Poems on Various Subjects, Religious and Moral* by Phillis Wheatley. The book was published in London in 1773.

Chapter 1

Phillis Wheatley

Little is known about Phillis Wheatley's early childhood. She was born in Eastern Africa (either Senegal[1] or Gambia[2]) sometime around 1753. At seven or eight years old, she was kidnapped and taken to America. She most likely was renamed for the slave ship the *Phillis*, which brought her to her new home.

She was purchased in 1761 by John Wheatley, a wealthy Boston merchant. He wanted to make her a household servant and companion to his wife, Susanna. John Wheatley already owned several slaves. But he wanted a young one who could do personal work for his wife. This would include fixing and delivering her medicine, water, or tea; fetching her bonnet; opening or closing doors; handling Mrs. Wheatley's fans during summer's heat; and keeping her fires alive during winter.

Phillis was so young when she arrived in Massachusetts that she was still losing her front baby teeth. The last of the enslaved lot from Senegal, she seemed frail. However the Wheatleys, drawn to her "humble and modest demeanor," took her home.[3]

The Wheatleys' daughter Mary taught Phillis to speak English. A sharp student, Phillis soon learned to read and write, too. John and Susanna Wheatley were impressed by their young servant's "uncommon intelligence." They also praised her kind nature and good manners.[4]

The Wheatleys brought Phillis up alongside their own daughters. She was allowed to spend her free time reading and writing. The Wheatleys seldom forced her to do hard labor around the house. Before long, Phillis even learned Latin and Greek.

Phillis never took the Wheatleys' kindness for granted. At home, she ate her meals at the family table. But when the Wheatleys took her with them to eat dinner in public, Phillis always asked to eat at a side table.[5]

Phillis studied the Bible and was baptized in the Wheatleys' church, the Old South Meeting House. She took her faith seriously. Much of her later poetry is religious.[6]

Her Career Begins

Phillis began writing poetry in her early teens. Though she never went to school, she knew Scripture and the classics. She also liked to read modern poetry. She wrote in the style of the popular British writers of the day.

The Wheatleys liked showing off how smart their young servant was. They introduced Phillis to many of Boston's most important families and clergymen. The Wheatleys' friends, in turn, started asking Phillis to write poems for them. Many of her first poems were elegies (poetic tributes to people who recently died).

Phillis published her first poem, "On Messrs. Hussey and Coffin," at the age of twelve or thirteen. In 1770 she wrote an elegy to famed preacher George Whitefield. That poem became extremely popular. Not only did readers in

Boston like it; people throughout the colonies read and admired it. Copies of the poem were even sent to England. Phillis went from being a "local celebrity" to a "poet with a reputation throughout the colonies and...overseas."[7]

Most of her poetry was uncontroversial. She never condemned slavery. She even wrote a poem that celebrated how being a slave brought her closer to Christ. In "On Being Brought from Africa to America," she wrote:

'Twas mercy brought me from my Pagan land,
Taught my benighted soul to understand

That there's a God, that there's a Savior too
Once I redemption neither sought nor knew...

Remember, Christians, Negros, black as Cain,
May be refin'd, and join th'angelic train.[8]

She did make a sad reference in one of her poems to being kidnapped as a child. But she only did so to create an image of intense suffering. In a 1772 poem addressed to Lord Dartmouth, she wrote:

I, young in life, by seeming cruel fate,
Was snatched from Afric's fancy'd happy seat:

What pangs excrutiating must molest,
What sorrows labour in my parent's breast?[9]

However, she didn't dwell on this sad picture. Instead, she compared her parents' sadness to the suffering of colonists living under Britain's oppressive rule. She expressed her hope that the American colonists would one day be free from England. Then she thanked Lord Dartmouth for his help in repealing the Stamp Act.[10]

Phillis lived a unique life. Her experiences at the Wheatley home differed from those of most African slaves living in America. Modern readers also must bear in mind that she was writing for an entirely white audience.

13

A Trip to England

Phillis's health was poor for most of her life. In 1773, on the advice of a family doctor, the Wheatleys sent Phillis to England in the care of their son. There she met "many individuals of distinction."[11] She most likely met Lady Huntington, who had sponsored the late Rev. George Whitefield (the man who inspired Wheatley's most famous poem).

Wheatley bought, or received as gifts, many books of poetry during her trip. She even took a tour of the Tower of London. She was delighted to see lions, panthers, and tigers in the Royal Menagerie at the tower. She also got to examine the crown jewels and the Royal Christening Font.[12]

While Wheatley was staying in London, her book *Poems on Various Subjects, Religious and Moral* was published in England. She dedicated the book to the Countess of Huntington.

It was rare in that time for any American to have a book of poetry published. It was almost unheard of for a woman to publish such a book. That Phillis Wheatley— a female, African-American slave—became a published author was astounding. It served as proof of the extraordinary public interest in her work.

However, many unbelieving readers suspected the poems were not Wheatley's original work. Her editor, therefore, placed a special preface in the book. It included a sworn statement by her master, and a separate statement signed by eighteen important Bostonians, declaring that she was the true author.[13]

Phillis Wheatley's brief stay in England marked the high point of her fame. She even was scheduled to be introduced to King George III at his court. However, before she could go, she was called back to America

14

Phillis Wheatley

This statue of Phillis Wheatley, sculpted by Meredith Bergmann in 2003, is part of the Boston Women's Memorial, which also includes statues of Abigail Adams and Lucy Stone.

to take care of her sick mistress.[14] Soon after Phillis returned to Boston in 1774, Mrs. Wheatley died.

Over the next few years, Phillis Wheatley wrote many patriotic poems inspired by the American Revolution. George Washington was so impressed by a poem she dedicated to him that he invited her to meet him.[15]

The years of the American Revolution were difficult for Phillis. Her owner, John Wheatley, died in 1778. He had freed Phillis shortly before his death. However, freedom was a mixed blessing. With no one to take care of her, she fell into poverty. Many of the Wheatleys' friends, who might have helped Phillis in her struggle for independence, were loyalists. They fled Boston after the war began, leaving Phillis even more alone.

Not long after the death of her former master, Wheatley married John Peters, an African-American grocer. He failed in several business attempts, and ended up in debtors' jail.[16] Meanwhile, Wheatley was unable to sell her poetry. Books of poetry were considered a luxury, and during the lean war years, nobody had the money to print or buy them. Wheatley became a domestic servant to support herself and her husband. As an independent adult, she finally had to perform the hard work from which the Wheatleys had spared her.

She gave birth to three children, but they all died young. The last died alongside her, and shared a funeral with her. Three days after Wheatley's death in December 1784, three of her poems were published. This was an honor, but it came too late to help provide the financial support she had desperately needed.[17] Her book of poetry, which caused such a sensation in England in 1773, was printed in the United States in 1793.[18]

Her Legacy

Phillis Wheatley's poetry is no longer widely read. Nevertheless, her status as the first published African-American author has made her name well known. At the time she wrote, she bore the burden of having to prove to white society that African Americans were capable of intellctual and artistic achievement. Many important thinkers of her time refused to treat her work as anything more than a curiosity. She forced them to consider the notion that African Americans had minds equal to those of white people.[19]

Today, Wheatley remains an inspiration to young African-American authors. Erin Aubry Kaplan, a contributing writer to both the *Los Angeles Times* and *Essence* magazine, wrote in December 2007:

> When I was in first grade, I wrote in an assignment that I wanted to be a 'poetess like Phillis Wheatley' when I grew up. I'd only seen one drawing of Phillis Wheatley, but it had made an impression…in the mid 1770's she'd somehow gone from being a slave to being a poet, who mastered complicated forms of poetry that had been the exclusive domain of the white folks who once owned her. This felt like the height of heroism to me, and I resolved to become a Phillis Wheatley in my time.[20]

Through the publication of her slim volume of poems, this often frail slave girl was the forerunner of future generations of African-American writers.

Phillis Wheatley Timeline

c. 1753—Phillis Wheatley is born, possibly in present-day Senegal or Gambia.

1761—She is kidnapped, brought by slave ship to Boston, and purchased by John Wheatley.

1770— "An Elegiac Poem, on the Death of the Celebrated Divine...George Whitefield" is published.

1773—Goes to London with Mr. Nathaniel Wheatley. Her book *Poems on Various Subjects, Religious and Moral* is published there.

1776—Meets George Washington.

1778—Phillis Wheatley is set free following the death of John Wheatley.

1778—Marries John Peters.

1784—Phillis Wheatley dies on December 5.

1834—*Poems of Phillis Wheatley* is published posthumously.

1864—*Letters of Phillis Wheatley, the Negro Slave-Poet of Boston* is published posthumously.

Chapter 2

Paul Laurence Dunbar

Paul Laurence Dunbar was a man of contradiction. He was widely admired during his short life for his poems written in African-American dialect. Yet he struggled to find readers for his beautiful poems written in standard English. He became a national celebrity, and made friends with many important people. But he died in poverty.[1] The popularity of his poems made African-American slang an acceptable form of expression. Modern poets who write in African-American speech patterns owe him a debt. But many scholars have criticized his work for pandering to white audiences. They accused Dunbar of presenting stereotypical "minstrel show" portrayals of African-American life.[2]

Dunbar was born in 1872 in Dayton, Ohio. His parents were both former slaves from Kentucky. They separated when he was young.

His mother, Matilda, worked as a washerwoman for many local families. The parents of Orville and Wilbur Wright paid her to do some of their cleaning. Matilda had fond memories of hearing poetry recited by the

Paul Laurence Dunbar

family she worked for when she was a slave. She strongly encouraged her own children to read and write poems.[3]

Dunbar was a standout at Dayton Central High School. He was the only African-American student in his class. Yet he rose to great heights. He was a member of the debating team and the editor of the school newspaper. He served as president of the school's literary society.[4] He also was elected president of his class and delivered the school's graduation poem in June 1891.[5]

After finishing high school, Dunbar wrote for several small Dayton newspapers. He published a short-lived African-American newspaper called the *Dayton Tattler*. His former classmates the Wright brothers helped finance the paper. But he relied on his job as an elevator operator to make ends meet.

Dunbar received an important gift on his twentieth birthday in 1892. The Western Association of Writers was having its convention in Dayton that day. One of Dunbar's former teachers invited him to give the welcome address. His speech made him a local celebrity. He published his first book of dialect poems, *Oak and Ivy*, that same year. He sold copies of it for a dollar apiece to the people who rode his elevator.[6]

Dunbar's fame began to spread. He was invited to recite his poems at the World's Fair in Chicago in 1893. There he met the famous abolitionist and author Frederick A. Douglass, who hailed Dunbar as "the most promising young colored man in America."[7]

Dunbar moved to Toledo after the fair. In 1895 he published his second book, *Majors and Minors*. It brought him national fame. A critic in the popular *Harper's Weekly* magazine praised his work. Afterward, a major New York publisher combined his two books and in 1896 printed them under the title *Lyrics of a Lowly Life*.[8] The name was

inspired by the English poet William Wordsworth's book of poems, *Lyrical Ballads*.[9] Dunbar was invited to England to recite his poems for London literary societies.[10]

Dunbar returned to America after his successful trip overseas. He toured the eastern United States giving poetry readings. He married the poet and scholar Alice Ruth Moore in 1898.

Dunbar's growing reputation helped him get a post as a clerk in the Library of Congress. He was awarded an honorary Master of Arts degree from Atlanta University.[11] Dunbar and his wife lived in Washington for just over a year. But their home briefly became a center for the District's African-American cultural life.

Ohio-born president William McKinley invited Dunbar to ride in his inaugural parade. It was an unprecedented honor for an African American.[12]

Dunbar continued to write poems in both dialect and standard English. But he also started writing fiction. He eventually published four books of short stories and four novels. Some people criticized his fiction for "pandering to popular racist images." But his final novel, *The Sport of Gods* (1903), took on a more challenging topic. It explored the problems faced by African Americans migrating from the rural south to the urban north.[13]

A Poet of Two Voices

The popularity of Dunbar's dialect poems became a problem. They brought him national, and even international, fame. But they blinded many readers to the power and beauty of his more traditional verses.

Some of Dunbar's better-known dialect poems include "A Negro Love Song" and "When Malindy Sings." A modern reader might find them silly at first glance. They repeat lines like a chorus. They tell simple stories.

"He sang of love when earth was young . . .," wrote Dunbar in "The Poet."

And they use old-fashioned African-American speech patterns that would sound racist if a white person said them today.

But they skillfully combine irony and emotional truth. Their rhythms are expressive and musical.[14] In "When Malindy Sings," the narrator calls out to everyone around him to be quiet, so that he can listen to Malindy's beautiful singing voice:

> Don't you hyeah de echoes callin'
>   F'om de valley to de hill?
>
> Let me listen, I can hyeah it,
>   Th'oo de bresh of angel's wings,
>
> Sof'an'sweet, "Swing Lo, Sweet Chariot,"
>
> Ez Malindy sings.[15]

A thoughtful reader may notice Dunbar's use of symbolism. He seems to be asking everyone to listen respectfully to the beauty of African-American speech. In fact, Dunbar attracted large audiences whenever he recited his dialect poems. By doing so, he opened the doors for generations of future African-American writers who wanted to write in their own cultural language.[16]

However, the white literary establishment had a hard time making sense of the two voices Dunbar used in his work. They thought of him first and foremost as a dialect poet. As a result, they did not pay much attention to his more traditional poems. Those poems, however, were exquisitely written. They are the works for which Dunbar is most famous today.[17]

One of his better-known poems is called "We Wear the Mask." It describes how African Americans need to present a pleasant face to the white community to be accepted. But it also describes their inward resentment:

24

With torn and bleeding hearts we smile...
Why should the world be over-wise,

In counting all our tears and sighs?
Nay, let them only see us, while

We wear the mask.[18]

Dunbar expresses similar ideas in his poem "Sympathy." He writes:

I know why the caged bird sings, ah me,
When his wing is bruised and his bosom sore,

When he beats his bars and would be free;
It is not a carol of joy or glee,

But a prayer that sends from his heart's deep core...[19]

As he grew older, Dunbar became increasingly aware of how his dialect poems overshadowed his other works. At times, he almost appeared ashamed of them.[20]

Untimely Death

Dunbar's final years were sad and difficult. He suffered from tuberculosis. There was no cure for it at the time. The disease lingered for many years and caused him to slowly waste away. His illness may have been made worse by the dusty conditions of his job at the Library of Congress. In 1902, he and his wife separated. He battled depression, alcoholism, and recurring bouts of pneumonia. But he continued to give poetry readings and write new work. He ultimately produced twelve books of poetry.

By 1904, his health was so poor that he could no longer speak in public. He returned to Dayton to live with his mother.[21] He died in 1906 at the age of thirty-three. In 1936, two years after his mother's death, the Dunbar House became the first state memorial in Ohio to honor an African American.[22]

25

Paul Laurence Dunbar Timeline

1872—Dunbar is born on June 27 in Dayton, Ohio.

1892—Gives the welcoming address to the Western Association of Writers.

1892—*Oak and Ivy* is published.

1893—Recites poetry at the World's Fair.

1895—*Majors and Minors* is published.

1896— *Lyrics of Lowly Life*, a collection of poems from his first two books, is published.

1897—Travels to England for a six-month poetry-reading tour.

1898—Marries Alice Ruth Moore, a writer, and works at the Library of Congress.

1899— *Lyrics of the Hearthside* and *Poems of Cabin and Field* are published.

1902—Dunbar and Moore separate.

1903—*The Sport of the Gods*, a novel, and *Lyrics of Love and Laughter*, a poetry collection, are published.

1905— *Howdy, Howdy, Howdy* and *Lyrics of Sunshine and Shadow* are published.

1906—Paul Dunbar dies on February 9 in Dayton, Ohio.

Langston Hughes

Langston Hughes is the best-known "African-American" poet. But even though his ancestors were mostly African, he was also descended from whites and Cherokee. In addition, he often traveled away from and lived outside of the United States for long periods. These diverse aspects of his life shaped Hughes. They gave him both an insider's view, and an outsider's view, of what it meant to be an "African American."

Born in Joplin, Missouri, in 1902 to James M. and Caroline Langston Hughes, childhood found him moving between homes in Kansas, Illinois, Ohio, and Mexico City.

Langston came from a distinguished family. His maternal grandmother's first husband fought with John Brown in the raid on Harpers Ferry and died there. Her second husband (Hughes's grandfather Charles Langston) had been an important Kansas politician during Reconstruction. Charles's brother John Mercer Langston (Hughes's great uncle) was once a member of Congress from Virginia. He was also the founding dean of Howard University's law school.[1]

Langston Hughes

Hughes's parents separated when he was still a baby. James Hughes was a light-skinned man of obvious mixed race. Leaving his family to fend for itself, he moved to Mexico to escape American Jim Crow laws. He became a successful businessman and landowner. Young Langston remained in the United States, shuttled between his mother's and his grandmother's homes. He grew up in near poverty.

His mother fought the school board to get him enrolled at an all-white elementary school in Topeka, Kansas, later the scene of a famous desegregation case. There, he was bullied by some students but defended by others. He said the experience taught him "very early in life that our race problem is not really of black against white, and white against black. It's a problem of people who are not very knowledgeable, or who have small minds, or small spirits."[2]

Langston started writing when he was very young. In eighth grade, he was named class poet. However, he later claimed he had never wanted to be a writer as a child. Two years before his death he said, "I thought I might like to be a doctor, you know, or else a streetcar conductor is what I most wanted to be."[3] His streetcar desires never came to pass. But he rode a lot of trains, trolleys, and buses when he was young. And he did a lot of traveling.

Langston moved to northern Ohio as a teenager. He regularly contributed poems and short stories to his high school literary magazine. He became yearbook editor at Cleveland's Central High School in 1920. He was even elected class poet again.[4] Although he was not friendless, he was a rather solitary young man, spending long hours in quiet thought.

After finishing high school, Langston took a train trip to Mexico to visit his father and persuade him to pay

29

for college. Looking out the window of his train car, he stared at the Mississippi River. He started thinking about the role that river had played in America's history of slavery. Then he started thinking about other rivers around the planet. They had also played a part in the history of slavery. He collected his thoughts in a poem entitled "The Negro Speaks of Rivers." His first published poem, it became his signature verse and played a significant role in African-American education.

His visit with his father did not go well. After many arguments, his father finally agreed to pay Langston's tuition at Columbia University in New York City. But he discouraged Langston from writing poetry. He urged him to study more practical subjects in college. He wanted him to become an engineer.

Hughes lasted only one year at Columbia, which at the time did not welcome blacks from the nearby Harlem neighborhood. But he fell in love with New York—especially Harlem. He traveled continually for the next few decades. But he always returned to Harlem. He soon came to think of it as his true home.

World Traveler

Hughes took several different jobs in his twenties to support himself while he wrote. Most didn't pay very well. He worked as a delivery boy and as a vegetable farmer. He served as a mess boy on a ship anchored in the Hudson River. In 1923 he joined the crew of a merchant steamboat traveling to Africa. The next year, he worked on another boat that was traveling to Europe. He jumped ship in Paris. He lived for a short while in the "City of Lights" and worked in the kitchen of a nightclub.[5]

Hughes eventually returned to the United States and moved to Washington, D.C. In 1929, he earned a

degree from Lincoln University in Pennsylvania. There he assisted Carter G. Woodson, founder of the Association of African Life and History and of Black History Week (now Black History Month). But working with Woodson interfered with his writing, so he left the association and took low-paying jobs in a laundry and in a restaurant. Ironically, this led him to meet renowned white poet Vachel Lindsay. It was Lindsay's public endorsement of Hughes's poetry that helped spread his fame beyond the African-American community.

Hughes took off traveling again as soon as he graduated. First he went to Haiti. Then he visited Russia. At the time, Russia was called the Soviet Union. Its communist government did not get along well with the United States. The American government discouraged its citizens from traveling there. Hughes went to Russia to work on a film about race relations in America. The project fell through. However, he remained in Moscow and enjoyed the lively theater scene. From there he traveled to China.

When Hughes finally returned to the United States, he lived in California. After his father died, he moved to Mexico to settle his father's business affairs. Further journeys took him back to Europe. He served as a news correspondent in Madrid during the Spanish Civil War.

Hughes spent the next several years shuttling between California, Ohio, and New York.[6] In 1947 he briefly became poet-in-residence at the University of Atlanta. But the next year he returned to Harlem, which he made his primary home for the rest of his life.[7]

31

Prolific Writer

When Hughes began writing, he made a deliberate decision to celebrate his racial heritage in his poetry. But

The Harlem Renaissance revolutionized the dynamics of African-American arts and literature in the United States.

this goal was not always easy. Hughes was born at a time when many African Americans tried to leave their heritage behind. They were tired of being poor. They were tired of being the victims of prejudice. They wanted to fit into mainstream society.

In a 1926 essay in *The Nation*, Hughes wrote, "This is the mountain standing in the way of any true Negro art in America—this urge within the race toward whiteness, the desire to pour racial individuality into the mold of American standardization, and to be as little Negro and as much American as possible."[8]

In 1921, Hughes published his first poem, "A Negro Speaks of Rivers," in W. E. B. Du Bois's magazine *The Crisis*. It immediately attracted the attention of the leading writers of the day. Soon afterward, the magazine began printing more of his poems. In January 1926, Knopf published his first collection of poetry, *Weary Blues*, to great acclaim.

The next year Knopf released his second book, *Fine Clothes to the Jew*. Though this book was also well received, many African Americans criticized it. They thought Hughes described the whole "blues culture" in an "unflattering" way.[9]

Throughout the 1920s and 1930s, Hughes was deeply involved in the artistic movement known as the Harlem Renaissance. This name describes the period of history when African-American artists and intellectuals truly came into their own. One of the goals of this movement was to celebrate the positive uniqueness of African-American culture. Writers and artists from this period challenged historic European and white American traditions and prejudices. They encouraged their fellow artists to express themselves on their own terms, and to explore their identities as African Americans.

33

The movement was based in Harlem. It included dozens of brilliant authors, poets, musicians, artists, and thinkers. Hughes's poetry became one of the best-known products of this era. Hughes also became the Harlem Renaissance's most visible spokesperson. He not only helped define the spirit of the age through his poems. He also established an historical record of the period with his autobiography *The Big Sea*, published in 1940.[10]

Unlike most of his contemporaries, Hughes continued to achieve remarkable success after the Harlem Renaissance ended. He published sixteen books of poetry. Two of his most famous are *Shakespeare in Harlem* (1942) and *Ask Your Mama: Twelve Moods for Jazz* (1961). He also wrote dozens of short stories, novels, screenplays, autobiographies, and dramas. He published many essays and even wrote a few children's books. In addition, he edited several anthologies of African-American writing.

Because Hughes was so well known, he received abundant praise during his lifetime. But he also drew criticism. Conservative political groups disapproved of his left-leaning politics, particularly his support of the American Communist party. However, the beauty of his poetry never ceased to attract enthusiastic readers.

Poet of Social Justice

Hughes's poems often deal with sad subjects. But sometimes he used humor in his writing to transcend the world-weary tone of his poems. He based the rhythms of his poems in the patterns of blues music. This gave his writing a melodic beat, which is pleasant to both read and hear.

In many of his poems, Hughes addressed the need for true racial equality. He often returned to the theme of how difficult it was for African Americans to succeed in an oppressive environment. In one of his most famous poems, "Harlem," he asks, "What happens to a dream deferred?" He begins his poem by wondering if "it dries up / like a raisin in the sun?" But then he hints at anger when he continues asking, "does it fester...stink...crust over...? Maybe it just sags / like a heavy load. / Or does it explode?"[11]

He expressed a sadder point of view when he told the story of a lonely piano player in "The Weary Blues":

...And far into the night he crooned that tune.
The stars went out and so did the moon.

The singer stopped playing and went to bed
While the Weary Blues echoed through his head.

He slept like a rock or a man that's dead.[12]

Yet his words were encouraging in his poem "Mother to Son." In it, a woman compares her life's journey to walking up a set of splintered, rugged stairs. She urges her child,

So boy, don't you turn back.
Don't you set down on the steps.

'Cause you finds it's kinder hard.
Don't you fall now –
For I'se still goin', honey,

I'se still climbin',
And life for me ain't been no crystal stair.[13]

A True Renaissance Man

Hughes lived through remarkably diverse experiences. He was a child of poverty and a grandchild of heroes. He was a restless world traveler and a proud resident of Harlem. A man of mixed race, he was accepted by the white community. He was a controversial figure who attracted

35

criticism. He drew upon these experiences to create an enormous body of complex and original work.

Toward the end of his life, Hughes was not only recognized as one of the most distinguished writers of the African-American experience. He also was considered one of America's most respected poets, regardless of race. His works had been translated into numerous foreign languages, ranging from Russian to Hindi.[14] Admirers nicknamed him the "O. Henry of Harlem" and the "Dean of Negro Writers in America." However, he particularly enjoyed (and even encouraged) the often-used title, "The Poet Laureate of the Negro Race."[15] He was awarded the National Association for the Advancement of Colored People (NAACP) Harmon gold medal in 1930 and its Spingarn Medal in 1960, and he became a member of the National Institute of Arts and Letters in 1961. He died in New York on May 22, 1967, following complications from cancer surgery.

Langston Hughes Timeline

1902—Hughes is born on February 1, in Joplin, Missouri.

1921—Hughes's poem "The Negro Speaks of Rivers" is published. He attends Columbia University for one year.

1924—Hughes moves to Washington, D.C.

1926—*The Weary Blues*, a book of poetry, and "The Negro Artist and the Racial Mountain," an essay, are published. Hughes attends Lincoln University in Pennsylvania.

1927—*Fine Clothes to the Jew*, a second book of poetry, is published.

1930—*Not Without Laughter*, Hughes's first novel, wins the Harmon gold medal for literature.

1931—*Dear Lovely Death*, a book of poetry, is published.

1935—Hughes's play *Mulatto* opens on Broadway.

1942—*Shakespeare in Harlem*, a book of poetry, is published.

1947—Hughes writes the lyrics for the musical *Street Scene*.

1949—*One-Way Ticket*, a book of poetry, is published.

1951—*Montage of a Dream Deferred*, a book of poetry, is published.

1956—*I Wonder as I Wander*, a book, is published.

1960—The NAACP awards Langston Hughes the Spingarn Medal for distinguished achievements by an African American.

1961—Hughes is inducted into the National Institute of Arts and Letters and publishes *Ask Your Mama: Twelve Moods for Jazz*, a collection of poetry.

1967—Hughes dies on May 22 in New York City.

Gwendolyn Brooks

Gwendolyn Brooks grew up in one of the worst neighborhoods of Chicago. Yet she had an important advantage that helped her rise above her poor surroundings: her strong family. Her mother, Keziah Wims Brooks, was a schoolteacher. Her father, David Anderson Brooks, had wanted to be a doctor. He didn't have the money to finish school, however. So he worked as a janitor instead. Together, they raised Gwendolyn and her younger brother, Raymond, in a home filled with love and encouragement. When they discovered their daughter's talent with words, they excused her from many household chores and set up a desk for her in a back room. There, she perfected her skills and pursued her dreams.

Brooks's life outside her home was not so happy. She was born in Topeka, Kansas, in 1917. Her family moved to Chicago's South Side when she was a baby. There she not only suffered the hardships faced by all poor African-Americans living in a white world, but she also felt rejected by many members of her own race

Gwendolyn Brooks poses with her first book of poems, *A Street in Bronzeville*.

"because she lacked social or athletic abilities, a light skin, and good grade hair."[1]

So she turned to the comfort of her private writing space. She wrote her first poem when she was seven. By age eleven, she regularly wrote her thoughts in a journal. When she was still a child, her mother took her to meet the poets James Weldon Johnson and Langston Hughes. They were visiting Chicago on a speaking tour. Hughes urged Gwendolyn to read modern poetry. He encouraged her to write on a disciplined, regular basis.[2]

"I felt I had to write," she told *Ebony* magazine. "Even if I had never been published, I knew that I would go on writing, enjoying it and experiencing the challenge."[3]

By an early age, she was published. In fact, she published almost seventy-five poems in the popular African-American newspaper *Chicago Defender* by the age of sixteen. She attended three high schools. She went to the mostly white Hyde Park High and the all-black Wendell Phillips High. But she graduated from the integrated Englewood High in 1935. She earned a degree in English from Wilson Junior College the next year.[4]

After finishing school, she worked as a cleaning woman and secretary to a "spiritual advisor" who sold potions and charms to tenement dwellers. In 1937 she became the publicity director of the local NAACP Youth Council. Two years later she married Henry Blakely. She gave birth to her first child, Henry, Jr., in 1940. Her daughter, Nora, was born in 1951.

41

Prize-Winning Poet

Brooks was a busy young mother. But she found time to go to poetry workshops in Chicago's South Side Community Art Center. She joined a mostly white group of poets affiliated with famed and influential Harriet Monroe's *Poetry: A Magazine of Verse*. In 1943 she won a poetry award from the Midwestern Writers' Conference. In 1945, she published her first collection of poems, *A Street in Bronzeville*. The poems described the daily life of African Americans in the poor neighborhoods of Chicago and in the Armed Forces during World War II. The ideas she wrote about in that book—family life, racism, poverty, war, and the quest for honor and contentment—became the major themes of her work for the next two decades.

Her book received many good reviews. Brooks was awarded a Guggenheim fellowship. Her second collection of poems, *Annie Allen* (1949), was even more highly praised. It ended up winning the Pulitzer Prize. Brooks was the first African-American writer to receive that honor. She followed up with an autobiographical novel, *Maud Martha* (1953). Her third collection of poetry, *The Bean Eaters*, came out in 1960.

In 1967 Brooks reached a turning point in life. She went to the Second Black Writers' Conference at Fisk University. She was deeply impressed with the energy and conviction of the poets she met from the black arts movement. When she returned home, her writing took off in a new artistic and political direction.

42

Until then, Brooks had written in more traditional poetic styles. She wrote ballads and sonnets. She sometimes even copied the centuries-old styles of British poets like Geoffrey Chaucer and Edmund Spenser.[5] But after the conference, she began to write more free verse. She started to include more African-American slang and rhythms of speech in her work. She even left her longtime mainstream publisher Harper & Row. She began to publish her poems through Broadside Press, a small company owned and operated by African-American poet Dudley Randall.[6]

Brooks wrote many books of poems after this turning point. They include *In the Mecca, Riot, Family Pictures, Beckonings, To Disembark, Primer for Blacks, Mayor Harold Washington and Chicago—The I Will City*, and *Blacks*. She also wrote several books of children's poetry. Some of her best-known children's books are *Bronzeville Boys and Girls, We Real Cool*, and *Young Poet's Primer*.[7]

Brooks spent most of her adult life giving lectures and poetry readings. Like her mother, she also taught. And she always did what she could to support the arts.

During her long life, she received seventy honorary degrees. She also won a lifetime achievement award from the National Endowment for the Arts, and the National Book Foundation Award for Distinguished Contribution to American Letters. In 1984, she was named the Jefferson Lecturer by the National Endowment for the Humanities. It was the U.S. government's highest honor for achievement in writing at the time. She also served as Consultant in Poetry to the Library of Congress from 1985 to 1986.[8]

A Story-Telling Poet

Many of Brooks's early poems told stories about individual people. But even though she wrote poetry instead of prose, her characters were as richly drawn as those found in many novels and plays. She wrote about her humble characters in grand poetic styles. This forced the reader to see the dignity of the poor slum dwellers she described. In "The Rites for Cousin Vit," for example, she used a sonnet to memorialize a fun-loving party girl who died young. The poem begins,

43

Hillary Rodham Clinton presents the First Ladies Salute First Women award to Gwendolyn Brooks, right, during the National First Ladies Library's awards ceremony in Washington, D.C., in 1999.

Carried her unprotesting out the door.
Kicked back the casket-stand. But it can't hold her,

That stuff and satin aiming to enfold her,
The lid's contrition nor the bolts before.[9]

The free verse Brooks used in her later writing was also very powerful. She often shocked the reader with a different type of ironic contrast. Brooks dedicated her poem "We Real Cool" to "The Pool Players: Seven at the Golden Shovel":

… We real cool. We
Left school. We

Lurk late. We
Strike straight. We

Sing sin. We
Thin gin. We

Jazz June. We
Die Soon.[10]

Because of her talent for telling stories and creating vivid characters, Brooks sometimes described herself as a journalist. In 1987 she told *Ebony*, "I've always thought of myself as a reporter. When people ask why I don't stop writing, I say, 'Look at what's happening in this world. Every day there's something exciting or disturbing to write about.' With all that going on, how could I stop?"[11]

Inspiring Future Generations

Brooks was named poet laureate for the state of Illinois in 1968. She took over the job after the death of the famous poet Carl Sandburg. As state poet laureate, she promoted literature in large and small communities. For more than

45

twenty years, she developed and organized poetry activities in the poorest areas of Chicago. She held the title until her death in 2000.[12]

Rita Dove, who followed in Brooks's footsteps by becoming the second African American to win the Pulitzer Prize for poetry, paid tribute to her predecessor in heartfelt testimony:

> As someone who, as a Black child, was educated in a literary tradition that seemed to have little use for my existence except as a caricature or in servitude and who, as a young person, came of age in a society where the discourse of the melting pot effectively translated into: 'Disappear into the mainstream or Else,' I knew that Gwendolyn Brooks was among the few who gave me the courage to insist on my own story. . . . Her shining example opened up new possibilities for me and generations of younger artists.[13]

Gwendolyn Brooks Timeline

1917—Gwendolyn Brooks in born in Topeka, Kansas, on June 7.

1936—Graduates from Wilson Junior College in Chicago.

1939—Marries Henry L. Blakeley.

1945—*A Street in Bronzeville*, a book of poetry, is published.

1950—Brooks wins a Pulitzer Prize for *Annie Allen*, a book of poetry she published the previous year.

1953—*Maud Martha*, a novel, is published.

1960—*The Bean Eaters*, a book of poetry, is published.

1968—Brooks is named poet laureate for the state of Illinois.

1985–1986—Brooks is the Consultant in Poetry to the Library of Congress.

1989—Wins a lifetime achievement award from the National Endowment for the Arts.

1990—Becomes a professor of English at Chicago State University.

2000—Gwendolyn Brooks dies on December 3 in Chicago.

Playwright, poet, and activist Amiri Baraka, born Everett LeRoi Jones

Amiri Baraka

The 1960s were a time of big changes for African Americans. Schools and neighborhoods became integrated. Job opportunities opened up. But the decade also was marked by much violence. Riots broke out in many cities. Racism remained a dangerous force. And several important African-American leaders were murdered, including Malcolm X and Rev. Martin Luther King, Jr.

Many African-American leaders in the civil rights movement preferred to use peaceful language in their speeches and writings. They hoped that gentle words would appeal to more enlightened members of the dominant white culture. Other leaders, however, were less patient with white society. They used strong, angry language to demand immediate social justice for all members of their race. Amiri Baraka falls into the second group.

Amiri Baraka was born in 1934 during the Great Depression. He grew up in a lower-middle-class neighborhood in Newark, New Jersey. Amiri's parents

49

(Colt Leroy and Anna Lois Jones) named him Everett LeRoi Jones, but he went by LeRoi.

Amiri came from a hardworking family. His relatives had left the South to escape racial violence. Before his grandfather left Alabama, his business had been burned down twice. After the family moved to New Jersey, his grandfather became involved in African-American Republican politics. However, he was injured in a mysterious accident. Baraka later said his grandfather never completely recovered "physically or spiritually."[1]

Amiri grew up in a little more comfort than many African Americans of his time. His father worked for the postal service. He also had a job as a forklift operator. His mother was a social worker.[2]

Amiri attended Barringer High School, a mostly white college prep school in Newark. He graduated with honors in 1951. But he was a restless young man. He once said, "When I was in high school, I used to drink a lot of wine, throw bottles around…just because I couldn't find anything to satisfy myself."[3]

He enrolled at Rutgers University in New Brunswick, New Jersey. However, he felt uncomfortable at the mostly white college. So he transferred to Howard University in Washington, D.C.

Although he enjoyed Sterling Brown's classes on jazz music, he didn't like Howard very much either. He thought it was too concerned with pleasing mainstream (white) society. He believed the college encouraged its students to "fit in" too much. He felt students should celebrate their African-American heritage instead.[4]

Baraka left Howard without earning a diploma. In 1954 he joined the Air Force. He served for three years as a gunner in Puerto Rico. In time, he was promoted to

sergeant. But someone accused him of having communist sympathies. Baraka was dishonorably discharged.[5]

In 1957, he moved to Greenwich Village in New York City. He worked at a record warehouse and started writing about jazz music.[6] His articles appeared in music magazines including *Downbeat*, *Metronome*, and the *Jazz Review*.[7] He also began studying comparative literature at Columbia University.[8]

"King of the Village"

Baraka first became famous for writing about music. In 1963 he put his articles together in a book called *Blues People: Negro Music in White America*. It is still considered one of the most important works of jazz criticism ever published.

But Baraka was intrigued by the theater too. By 1964, he had written four plays. One of them, *The Dutchman*, won the Obie Award for Best American Off-Broadway Play of 1963–1964.[9]

During this period, he also became interested in poetry. In 1958, he set up a small publishing company called Totem Press. He and his first wife, Hettie Cohen, started printing *Yugen*, an art magazine. It featured writings by beat poets such as Allen Ginsberg.[10] Baraka soon began writing poetry too.

His first book of poetry came out in 1961. It was called *Preface to a Twenty-Volume Suicide Note*. Many of the poems in *Preface* compared childhood innocence with adult experience. Others were inspired by art, blues music, or his feelings for his wife.[11]

He was very influenced by the beat poets. He used their "stream of consciousness" writing style. Ideas in stream of consciousness poems often appear in long, run-on phrases or sentences. Baraka tried to make his poems sound like "thoughts" transferred directly from his mind to the paper. Poets who write in this style try not to use the "artificial" constraints of traditional poetry. They usually avoid rhymes and forced rhythms.

Baraka also was influenced by the Black Mountain poets of the late 1950s. The Black Mountain writers emphasized the sound of poetry read aloud. Baraka had always been interested in music and theater. It was an easy step for him to start giving poetry readings. He had a natural talent for performing. His poetry readings soon became very popular.

Baraka was now involved in many parts of New York's art scene. He wrote poetry and plays. He wrote about art and music. He was friends with many other artists in Greenwich Village. And his fame spread quickly, leading to his new nickname, "The King of the Village." The nickname was also a pun on his name LeRoi (which means "king" in French).[12]

A New Name

As the 1960s progressed, Baraka's interests started moving beyond the arts. He had always been fascinated by politics. He strongly believed in racial equality. His wife Hettie was a white, Jewish woman. As a couple, they socialized with people of all races. But as the civil rights movement took off, Baraka began to focus more on his African-American identity.

52

He was inspired by the great African-American leaders Malcolm X and Martin Luther King, Jr. But he was also impressed by the political artists and writers he had met in Cuba. He had visited that country in 1960 after the publication of his poem "January 1, 1959: Fidel Castro." In his autobiography, Baraka said, "Cuba split me open." He claimed the trip was "a turning point in my life."[13]

After the 1965 murder of Malcolm X, Baraka dropped his beat poet identity. He moved from Greenwich Village to Harlem. He divorced his wife Hettie and left their two children.

He embraced the new idea of black liberation. He became involved in the black nationalist movement. Wanting to reconnect with his African roots, he rejected his old name, LeRoi Jones. It sounded too much like a white man's name. He started using a new African name: Imamu Amiri Baraka.

He began giving open-air performance art shows based on his writings. With friends, he started a small theater. They called their organization the Black Arts Repertory Theater, or BART. They hoped BART would "create an art that would be a weapon in the Black Liberation Movement."[14] BART only lasted for a short time, but Baraka soon became involved in other theater projects.

The Black Arts Movement

In 1967, Baraka moved back to Newark. He once again established a community theater. He called his new stage the Spirit House. He wanted it to support African-American arts. He continued to be politically active. He organized supporters to help elect Newark's first African-American mayor.[15]

His poetry became increasing political. His second and third books of poems were called *The Dead Lecturer* and *Black Magic*. They included a lot of violent imagery. Baraka took a radical stand in his writing. He didn't just lament the sad conditions of African-American life. He didn't express a gentle hope that things might

Amiri Baraka is pictured in Newark, New Jersey, in 2002, after becoming the state's poet laureate.

improve. Instead, he urged African Americans to demand change *now*. Some of his poems even seemed to encourage African Americans to use force to get what they deserved.

In 1967, Baraka and two friends were stopped by Newark police officers. The officers charged the three men with unlawfully carrying firearms and resisting arrest. Baraka claimed the guns were planted on him.

The resulting trial was controversial. It was overseen by an all-white jury. Baraka's poem "Black People" was admitted into evidence. The provocative poem urges poor people to take their fair share of America's material wealth.[16] Prosecutors suggested that Baraka was encouraging people to steal and use violence. Baraka's lawyers argued that it was unfair to admit a piece of art as evidence in a trial. Baraka was convicted. However, the verdict was overturned on appeal.

His provocative poems and controversial trial brought Baraka great fame. By the late 1960s, he was one of the best-known African-American writers of his day. However, he was not alone in writing confrontational poems. Many other African-American poets and artists joined him in writing aggressively about social issues. This trend became known as the black arts movement.

In 1968, Baraka co-edited *Black Fire: An Anthology of Afro-American Writing*. The book collected the work of many writers from the black arts movement. Baraka boldly proclaimed in the foreword to the book:

> These are the founding Fathers and Mothers, of our nation. We rise...by the power of our beliefs, by the purity and strength of our actions....These descriptions will be carried for the next thousand years, of good, and of evil. These will be the standards black men make reference to for the next thousand years.[17]

55

More and more African-American artists began to write poems. The literary establishment took notice. When Boston University professor Willis Wager described the literary scene of the early 1970s, he called Baraka "a leading figure among black poets today." He also noted that "among black authors there was more of a tendency to write poetry than fiction—thus perpetuating in some ways the tradition of the Harlem Renaissance in the 1920s, but carrying it on into a more distinctly black type of expression."[18]

Musical Verses

Baraka's poetry is often confrontational. He likes to use stark images and hard sounds. However, he blends them together in a musical way. For example, he begins his poem "Return of the Native":

> *Harlem is vicious*
> *modernism, BangClash.*
>
> *Vicious the way it's made.*
> *Can you stand such beauty?*[19]

He also writes about political topics. His "Poem For Black Hearts" was inspired by the death of Malcolm X:

> *...For all of him, and all of yourself, look up,*
> *black man, quit stuttering and shuffling, look up,*
>
> *black man, quit whining and stooping, for all of him,*
>
> *For Great Malcolm a prince of the earth,*
>
> > *let nothing in us rest*
>
> *until we avenge ourselves for his death...* [20]

56

Much of his writing appears angry. However, he sometimes writes inspirational poetry. He shows his softer side when he addresses a child in his emotional poem "Young Soul":

*First, feel, then feel, then
read, or read, then feel, then*

*fall, or stand, where you
already are...*

*Make some muscle
in your head, but*

*use the muscle
in yr heart.*[21]

No Quiet Retirement

In 1967, Baraka married his second wife, the poet Sylvia Robinson. She also changed her name in the late 1960s, to Amina Baraka. Amiri and Amina Baraka had five children together. But they have also remained active in Newark's art scene. Together, they established the word-music art ensemble Blue Ark: The Word Ship. They are presently codirectors of Kimako's Blues People, the "artspace" housed in their basement theater.[22]

As the 1970s progressed, Baraka began to distance himself from black nationalism. In 1974, he became a Third World Marxist. Under this new philosophy, he no longer criticized white people on principle. Instead, he condemned any "first-world oppressors" who tried to take away the rights of the poor.

To show his commitment to this new belief, he stopped using the title Imamu in his name. He decided that the word, which means "spiritual leader" in Swahili, gave a bad impression. He didn't want others to think he was placing himself above them.[23]

In addition to writing, Baraka has worked as a teacher. He has lectured at many colleges, including Yale, Columbia, San Francisco State, and George Washington universities. In 1979, he joined the faculty of the

57

State University of New York (SUNY) in Stony Brook, New York. He taught in the Africana Studies department. He retired in 2000. However, he continues to return to the campus to give popular poetry readings and performance art demonstrations.[24]

Baraka has published more than forty volumes of poetry and prose, including many plays and works of fiction. He has collected his essays and poems into numerous volumes. And he has written the lyrics to songs that have been used in plays and musicals. Love of music remains dear to his heart. Its influence is seen throughout his writing. "Poetry is music," he once said, "and nothing but music. Words with musical emphasis."[25]

At an age when most people have retired, Baraka continues to stir up controversy. In recognition of his lifelong contribution to the arts, he was named the poet laureate of the state of New Jersey. But after the September 11, 2001, attacks on the United States, he wrote a poem titled "Somebody Blew Up America." The controversial work caused a scandal. The governor of New Jersey asked Baraka to resign his post. When Baraka refused, the state legislature voted to eliminate the poet laureate position altogether.

Amiri Baraka's urgent writing serves as proof that the arts can make a difference in the lives of the poor. In the hands of an uncompromising artist such as Baraka, poetry can be a dangerous force to be reckoned with.

Amiri Baraka Timeline

1934—Born Everett LeRoi Jones on October 7 in Newark, New Jersey.

1954—Earns his BA in English from Howard University.

1954–1957—Serves in the U.S. Air Force.

1958—Marries Hettie Cohen and founds Totem Press.

1961—*Preface to a Twenty-Volume Suicide Note*, a book of poetry, is published.

1964—*Dutchman*, a play, is produced. It wins an Obie Award.

1965—Baraka and Cohen divorce. Baraka founds the Black Arts Repertory Theatre in Harlem.

1967—Marries Sylvia Robinson, who later changes her name to Amina Baraka.

1968—Becomes a Muslim and changes his name to Imamu Amiri Baraka.

1969—*Great Goodness of Life*, a play, is performed Off-Broadway.

1972—Baraka is one of the main organizers of the National Black Political Convention held in Indiana.

1974—Drops "Imamu" from his name, and adopts a Marxist philosophy.

1985—Becomes a professor of Africana Studies at the State University of New York in Stony Brook.

Jay Wright

Jay Wright

More than any other modern African–American poet, Jay Wright brings a multicultural understanding to his writing. He grew up in the Southwest. There he was introduced to American Indian and Hispanic customs. He lived and worked in Mexico and Europe as a young man. Those international experiences opened his eyes to a larger worldview. As he grew older, he studied ancient African religions. They inspired him to search for the roots of African–American traditions. These diverse aspects of his background have helped Wright to create complex and often scholarly poems. His poetry explores today's African–American experience within the context of its past and future.

Jay Wright was born in Albuquerque, New Mexico, in 1935. His father, George Murphy Wright, was American Indian and African American. His mother, born Leona Daily, was primarily African American. They separated when he was three years old. Jay was brought up by a guardian.

At fourteen, Jay moved to San Pedro, California. He lived there with his father while attending high school.

Afterward, he enrolled in the University of New Mexico, where he studied chemistry.[1]

Jay was a talented student. But he was also a gifted athlete. He especially loved baseball. He briefly played catcher for a St. Louis Cardinals farm team. Though he never played in the major leagues, he remained a lifelong lover of the sport.

Wright wrote about baseball in a 1969 article for *Sports Illustrated*. He described the sport as "the realization, the summit of a masculine esthetic." He said that by perfecting his skills, a ballplayer can transcend his limitations. Wright even compared baseball to art. He suggested that "Baseball offers the ballplayer what any man can learn of art, and of his life as art."[2]

Wright joined the army in the mid-1950s. He served in Germany in the Medical Corps. During his three-year tour of duty, he visited many parts of Europe. After leaving the army, he returned to the United States to finish college, earning a bachelor's degree from the University of California at Berkeley.

In 1961, Wright won a Rockefeller Brothers Theological Fellowship. He used the scholarship money to study at Union Theological Seminary in New York City. Afterward he went to Rutgers University in New Jersey, earning a master's degree in comparative literature in 1967.

The following year, he received a Woodrow Wilson/ National Endowment for the Arts fellowship. He used that grant money to tour the southern United States. He published a small booklet of poems, *Death as History*, in 1967. He also wrote two plays, which were produced and earned good notices. Princeton University honored him with a playwriting fellowship in 1970. Later honors include a Guggenheim Fellowship and a $500,000 MacArthur Foundation "genius grant."

During this time, many African-American writers became involved in the black arts movement. Wright never embraced the movement's angry and political writing style. But he was still deeply moved by the racial conflicts of the 1960s and early 1970s.

In 1968, Wright's dear friend and fellow poet Henry Dumas was killed. He was shot by a New York City policeman in a tragic case of mistaken identity. Wright wrote a heartfelt introduction to a book of Dumas's poems that was published after his death. In his prologue, he paid tribute to his fallen friend. He praised Dumas for celebrating the uniqueness of African-American language:

> The language of the Black community, as with that of any other group, takes its form, its imagery, its vocabulary, because Black people want them that way. Language can protect, exclude, express value, as well as assert identity. That is why Dumas' language is the way it is. In the rhythm of it, is the act, the unique manner of perception of a Black man.[3]

A Scholarly Poet

Wright enjoyed traveling when he was in the army. He continued to travel after he finished school. He worked in Mexico from 1968 to 1971. Afterward, he spent two years teaching at Dundee University in Scotland.

Between his two international trips, he published his first major collection of poetry, *The Homecoming Singer*. It was widely praised by critics. Wright put his extensive travel experience to use in his poems, creating many different and well-defined settings. But his detailed descriptions weren't just meant to be pretty backgrounds. They served as symbols for the people and ideas he wrote about.[4]

63

In the early 1970s, Wright began studying African religions. He published his next two poetry books in 1976. They were called *Soothsayers and Omens* and *Dimensions in History*. Both books used images from African mythology. The poems explored themes of individual growth and spiritual quests.

Wright was interested in many other subjects too. He studied the philosophy of science and anthropology. He read European literature from the Middle Ages and the Renaissance. He included references to many of these ideas in his poems. Reviewers of his books often remarked upon Wright's extensive scholarship. They also praised the way he used multiple layers of symbols.[5]

His next book, *The Double Invention of Komo*, came out in 1980. It is a series of poems that follows the Komo initiation rite of Africa's Bambara people. Reviewers have called it Wright's most ambitious book.[6]

Since writing *Komo*, Wright has published three more books of poetry: *Explications/Interpretations*, *Elaine's Book*, and *Boleros*.

In 2000, Wright collected his previously published works in a single volume of poetry, *Transfigurations: Collected Poems*. It was widely praised. In his review of the book, Washington University Professor Steven Meyer called Wright the "unsung wonder of contemporary American poetry."[7]

Wright's books continue to draw attention. But he likes to live away from the spotlight. He has worked as a teacher and poet-in-residence at many universities over the years. But he prefers to spend his time writing plays and poems at home. He and his wife Lois live quietly in New England. In 2008 he published five more books of poetry. Among the most recent are *The Guide Signs: Book One and Book Two* (2007) and *The Presentable Art of*

Reading Absence (2008). Some critics have seen him as a peer of T. S. Eliot and Walt Whitman, great icons of American cultural history.

Connecting With Roots

Wright often writes about the need for African Americans to reconnect with their history. In "The Albuquerque Graveyard," found in *Soothsayers and Omens*, he states:

> *I am going back*
> *to the Black limbo,*
>
> *of unwritten history*
> *of our own tensions.*
>
> *The dead lie here*
> *in a hierarchy of small defeats.*[8]

He also writes on religion and mythology. Sometimes he considers the role God plays in the lives of African Americans. In "Meta-A and the A of Absolutes," he writes:

> *Brown by day and black by night,*
> *my God has wings that open to no reason.*
>
> *He scutters from the touch of old men's eyes,*
> *scutters from the smell of wisdom, an orb*
>
> *of light leaping from a fire.*
> *Press him he bleeds.*[9]

No single theme connects Wright's works. He blends ideas from too many different traditions. However, the variety of his poems makes them interesting. He may be inspired by ancient religions one day and baseball the next. The poems he writes are thoughtful and complex, embracing blues, jazz, Caribbean, and Latin elements.

In a 1984 interview, Wright said, "A young man, hearing me read some of my poems, said that I seemed to be trying to weave together a lot of different things.

65

© Photographs by Diane Krajenski

In 2005, Kean University in Union, New Jersey, inducted students into Sigma Tau Delta, the Internationl English Honors Society. Jay Wright joined the celebration by reading a selection of his poetry.

My answer was that they are already woven, I'm just trying to uncover the weave."[10]

The image of a weaver is a good one for Wright. The Academy of American Poets seems to agree. Every April, this national organization celebrates National Poetry Month. In 2008, the Academy chose lines from a Jay Wright poem to put on its poster. The words came from the closing stanza of his poem, "The Healing Improvisation of Hair":

> *I carried my life, like a stone,*
> *in a ragged pocket, but I*
>
> *had a true weaving song, a sly*
> *way with rhythm, a healing tone.*[11]

67

Jay Wright Timeline

1935—Wright is born in Albuquerque, New Mexico.

1961—Earns his BA from the University of California.

1967—Completes his master's degree in comparative literature and publishes *Death as History*, a chapbook of poetry.

1968—Receives a Woodrow Wilson/National Endowment for the Arts Poets-in-Concert fellowship.

1971—*The Homecoming Singer* is published.

1980—*The Double Invention of Komo* is published.

1984—*Explications/Interpretations* is published.

1986—*Elaine's Book* is published.

1991—*Boleros* is published.

1996—Receives the Academy of American Poets Fellowship.

2000—Wins the Lannan Literary Award for Poetry.

2005—Receives Yale University's Bollingen Prize for American Poetry.

2007—*The Guide Signs Book One and Book Two* is published.

2008— *The Presentable Art of Reading Absence and Polynomials and Pollen: Parables, Proverbs, Paradigms,* and *Praise for Lois* are published.

Nikki Giovanni

People often think poetry is elitist. Even people who love to read sometimes think it's a snobbish or confusing art form. The general public seldom embraces it. Few poets draw large crowds to their poetry readings. Fewer still see their books appear on best-seller lists.

Nikki Giovanni, however, knows how it feels to be a popular poet. She uses a natural rhythm in her poems that sounds like the spoken word. She writes about topics with a broad, newsworthy appeal. By doing so, she has brought poetry to the people. In turn, she has attracted a large and devoted group of admirers that other poets could only dream about.

Nikki Giovanni was born in Knoxville, Tennessee, in 1943. She was named Yolande Cornelia Giovanni, Jr., after her mother. Her sister nicknamed her "Nikki" when she was just a child. She once joked that she got her unusual last name because her ancestors "had an Italian slave master."[1] When she was young, her family moved to Cincinnati. They settled in a mostly African-American neighborhood.

Nikki Giovanni leads the crowd in a cheer after closing remarks at a 2007 convocation to honor the victims of the shooting rampage at Virginia Tech University.

A talented student, Nikki graduated from high school one year early.[2] She enrolled in Fisk University in Nashville, Tennessee, where her grandfather had gone. A few months after starting classes, she was expelled. She had left campus to visit her grandparents for Thanksgiving, but neglected to get her dean's permission first.

She returned to her parents' home and worked at a Walgreens. Because she didn't want to fall behind in school, she took some classes at the University of Cincinnati. In 1964, she went back to Fisk. She graduated with high honors in 1967, earning a degree in history.[3]

While at Fisk, Giovanni developed an interest in writing. She edited the school's literary magazine, *Elan*. She joined writers' workshops and through them met outstanding poets including LeRoi Jones, Margaret Walter Alexander, Melvin Tolson, John Oliver Killens, and Dudley Randall. She also became involved in the growing civil rights movement, helping to restore Fisk's chapter of the Student Nonviolent Coordinating Committee, the college arm of Rev. Martin Luther King, Jr.'s Southern Christian Leadership Conference.

After graduating, Giovanni returned home to Ohio. For her first job out of college, she planned and directed Cincinnati's first Black Arts Festival in 1967.

A Star Is Born

The 1968 assassination of Martin Luther King, Jr., had a deep effect on Giovanni. Shortly after his death, she wrote her first book of poems. She borrowed money and paid to publish it herself. It was called *Black Feeling Black Talk*. The poems were about the civil rights movement. During its first year in print, it sold more than ten thousand copies! The Harlem Council of the Arts published her next book, *Black Judgement*. It drew even more praise.

71

To promote her books, Giovanni traveled to New York City to give a poetry reading at an arts festival. She spoke in front of an enthusiastic standing-room-only crowd at the popular jazz club Birdland.[4] The next day, the *New York Times* reviewed her performance, noting that she was "the only attraction to outdraw James Brown."[5]

So began her career as a poet and speaker. Soon she started writing essays and children's books too. Popular magazines introduced her work to increasingly large audiences. *Ebony* named her its Woman of the Year in 1970. The next year, *Mademoiselle* followed suit. In 1972, *Ladies' Home Journal* gave her the same honor. In a foreword to Giovanni's 1972 collection of poems *My House*, editor Ida Lewis called the author "the Princess of Black Poetry."[6] Giovanni continued to draw large, admiring crowds everywhere she spoke. In 1971, with the backing of an orchestra, she presented her poem "Truth Is On Its Way" to an audience of fifteen hundred.

At first, Giovanni was best known for her poems about civil rights and racial politics. But she also dealt with women's issues. Her strong belief that she—an African-American woman—could stand on her own as a writer struck a chord with female readers throughout the country. Her interest in feminist causes mixed freely with her concerns about African-American issues. She became an active member of the National Council of Negro Women in 1972.

In 1969 she gave birth to her only child, Thomas Watson Giovanni. She chose to have her son out of wedlock because she believed that marriage was often not good for women. "I had a baby at twenty-five because I *wanted* to have a baby and I could *afford* to have a baby," she told *Ebony*. "I did not get married because I didn't *want* to get married, and I could *afford* not to get married."[7]

Though her independent views are more common today, they seemed radical to many people at the time. In fact, her own father began sending her money after her son was born. He assumed that with no man to support her, she needed financial help. So on her next trip to Cincinnati, Giovanni deliberately left one of her royalty checks out on a table for her father to see. "He said, 'Is that for you?'" she recalled. When she said that it was, he admitted, "You're doing all right. You don't need my money."[8]

While Giovanni continued to write, she also began her teaching career in the late 1960s. She first worked as an assistant professor of black studies for Queens College of the City University of New York in 1968. Since then, she has taught at several colleges and universities. These include Rutgers, Ohio State, the College of Mount St. Joseph in Cincinnati, and Texas Christian University. Since 1989, she has been a tenured professor at Virginia Tech in Blacksburg, Virginia.

A Poet of the Spoken Word

Giovanni's poetry uses powerful imagery—and sometimes rough language—to create a strong sense of emotion. She also is quick to criticize public figures and social conventions. She explained to *Cincinnati* magazine, "Poetry has always been a bellwether and it always will be. I can't imagine a world where there's not at least one good poet saying things like, 'You people suck.'" She admitted that there will always be popular writers who will praise whatever "king" is in power. But she added, "The king needs to be picked on. And that's what poets do."[9]

Her tribute to Martin Luther King, Jr., for example, is more confrontational than sentimental. Giovanni

Nikki Giovanni is pictured with her son, Thomas, on her shoulders at the Operation PUSH Soul Picnic at the 142nd St. Armory, New York City, March 26, 1972.

contrasts his famous "I Have a Dream" speech with an urgent plea to create a safe and fair world for African Americans:

> His headstone said
> FREE AT LAST, FREE AT LAST
>
> But death is a slave's freedom
> We seek the freedom of free men
>
> And the construction of a world
> Where Martin Luther King could have lived and
>
> preached non-violence[10]

Giovanni writes with a natural-sounding rhythm. She once explained that she grew up in a family of good storytellers. "I appreciated the quality and the rhythm of the telling of the stories, and I know when I started to write that I wanted to retain that—I didn't want to become the kind of writer that was stilted or that used language in ways that could not be spoken. I use a very natural rhythm; I want my writing to sound like I talk."[11]

It is easy to imagine a speaker reciting her poem, "Nikki-Rosa," which begins:

> childhood remembrances are always a drag
> if you're Black
>
> you always remember things like living in Woodlawn
> with no inside toilet...[12]

In fact, the appealing "vocal" quality that Giovanni brings to her writing has not only made her a popular figure at poetry readings. She also has become an award-winning spoken-word recording artist as well. Over the years, she has made many recordings of her work. Sometimes she records with gospel choirs and other musical backing.[13]

Still a Timely Poet

Long after many of her fellow writers from the black arts movement have retired, Giovanni keeps busy. In addition to publishing more than thirty books, she has collected dozens of honorary awards from universities, state art councils, and literary societies. In 2005, she was named one of Oprah Winfrey's "25 Living Legends." An admiring scientist even named a new species of bat for her![14]

In 2007, she returned to the national spotlight. She was asked to speak at a memorial service for the Virginia Tech students and teachers killed in a massacre. Her poem brought a sense of hope to the sad ceremony as she chanted:

> ...*We are Virginia Tech.*
> *We are Hokies.*
>
> *We will prevail*
> *We will prevail*
>
> *We will prevail.*
> *We are Virginia Tech.*[15]

Nikki Giovanni Timeline

1943— Born Yolande Cornelia Giovanni, Jr., on June 7 in Knoxville, Tennessee.

1967—Graduates from Fisk University and enrolls in the University of Pennsylvania's School of Social Work with the help of a Ford Foundation fellowship.

1968—*Black Feeling Black Talk*, a book of poetry, is self-published.

1969—*Black Judgement*, a book of poetry, is self-published. Giovanni's son, Thomas Watson Giovanni, is born.

1971—*Gemini*, an autobiography, and *Spin a Soft Black Song*, a book of poems for children, are published.

1972—*My House* is published. Giovanni joins National Council of Negro Women.

1973—*Ego Tripping and Other Poems for Young Readers* is published.

1974—*A Poetic Equation: Conversations Between Nikki Giovanni and Margaret Walker* is published.

1975—*The Women and the Men* is published.

1978—*Cotton Candy on a Rainy Day* is published.

1983—*Those Who Ride the Night Winds* is published.

1987—Giovanni becomes a professor of English and Gloria D. Smith professor of Black Studies at Virginia Tech, and is the subject of *Spirit to Spirit*, a documentary.

1996—Receives the Langston Hughes award for Distinguished Contributions to Arts and Letters.

2004—Giovanni is Poet-in-Residence at the Walt Whitman Birthplace.

2007—*Jimmy Grasshopper Versus the Ants*, a children's book; *Acolytes*, a book of poetry; and *On My Journey Now: Looking at African-American History Through the Spirituals*, a nonfiction book, are published.

2008—*Lincoln and Douglas: An American Friendship* with illustrator Bryan Collier and *Bicycles: Love Poems* are published.

Rita Dove

Today's African-American poets follow a long line of distinguished writers. Rita Dove, the first African American to be named Poet Laureate of the United States, once said:

> I feel a part of a literary family, a community of both living and dead poets. In the way of families, I may argue vehemently with other relatives sometimes, but the empathy—the fact of inclusion—is always there. I feel a deep affinity with Langston Hughes and Gwendolyn Brooks and Richard Wright—indeed, with what one would call the African-American canon of literature.[1]

Many of the African-American poets who came before Dove made racial issues the main theme of their work. Dove, however, often does not. She explained to the *Washington Post*, "Obviously as a black woman, I am concerned with race....But certainly not every poem of mine mentions the fact of being Black. There are poems about humanity, and sometimes humanity happens to be black."[2]

Rita Dove was born in 1952 in Akron, Ohio. Her father, Ray, became the first African-American research

Rita Dove

chemist to be hired by the tire and rubber industry—after operating an elevator at Goodyear while holding a Master of Arts degree. He was a member of the generation of well-educated African Americans that helped break down race barriers in American business. His example inspired his children to believe they too could accomplish their dreams.

He and Rita's mother, Elvira, tried to shield their four children from discrimination. They believed the best way their children could succeed was to get a good education. Dove has called her mother and father her biggest influences. She once said, "My parents instilled in us the feeling that learning was the most exciting thing that could happen to you, and it never ends."[3] Rita's older brother and two younger sisters pursued careers in science and mathematics. But she was drawn to literature. Still, "all of us love to read," she insisted.[4]

Dove's teachers also had a big influence on her. She has publicly thanked many of her teachers over the years for challenging and encouraging her. One particular teacher left a big impression. She brought Rita to a book signing during her senior year of high school.

"That's when I saw my first live author," Dove recalled. "To have someone actually in the same room with me, talking, and you realize he gets up and walks his dog the same as everybody else, was a way of saying, 'It is possible. You can really walk through that door too.'"[5]

Before that day, she thought of authors as being somehow above her. But at the reading she saw with her own eyes that they were just human. She realized then that she might actually become one herself.

Dove's childhood home was filled with books. Her parents encouraged their children to make regular

81

visits to the local library. "The library was the one place we got to go without asking...for permission," she recalled. "And what was wonderful about that was the fact that they let us choose what we wanted to read for extra reading material. So it was a feeling of having a book be mine entirely, not because someone assigned it to me, but because I chose to read it."[6]

One book Rita found especially interesting was an anthology of poetry. She found it in the library when she was about eleven. It started with poems from the ancient Roman era. It ended with poems from the 1950s. In between was a collection of the best poems written over the past two thousand years.

She read through the book as she saw fit. She spent more time on the poets she liked best. Slowly, she worked her way through the difficult words of writers most children would never try to read. Since she chose the book herself, nobody stopped to tell her it was too hard for her to understand. "And that's how my love affair...with poetry began," she said.[7]

Rita was an exceptional student in school. She worked hard and earned good grades. She played cello in her high school orchestra. She also led her school's majorette squad. In 1970, she finished Buchtel High School in Akron, Ohio, and was named one of the hundred most outstanding high school students in America. She was invited to the White House as a Presidential Scholar.

In 1973 she graduated with highest honors and a Phi Beta Kappa key from Miami University in Oxford, Ohio. She earned her degree in English. Afterward, she studied for two years in Tubingen, Germany, on a Fulbright scholarship.

Rita Dove, left, shakes hands with Judge J. Harvie Wilkinson III, right, after being appointed poet laureate of Virginia, September 20, 2004.

When she returned to the United States, she went to the University of Iowa. She joined the school's Writers' Workshop. She received her master's degree in 1977. While she was in Iowa, she met another Fulbright Scholar, a German writer named Fred Viebahn. They married in 1979. Their daughter, Aviva, was born in 1983.

A Pulitzer Prize

Dove taught creative writing at Arizona State University from 1981 to 1989. During those years, she also began publishing her poems in national magazines. Her first book of poetry, *The Yellow House on the Corner*, came out in 1980. Her second, *Museum*, followed in 1983. Her third collection, *Thomas and Beulah*, was published in 1986. It won the 1987 Pulitzer Prize for poetry. Dove was the second African-American poet to win that award, after Gwendolyn Brooks in 1950.

In a 1995 interview, Dove remembered the afternoon she heard about the prize. She had taken the day off work to plan her husband's 40th birthday party. She told her coworkers not to bother her. When the chairman of her department telephoned, she tried to hang up on him. She thought, "He's not supposed to disturb me! This is my day!" But then he told her about the prize. She could hardly believe it. She later said, "I really felt like…the camera lights came on into my life. It was quite distinct."[8]

Thomas and Beulah is a series of poems inspired by Dove's grandparents, Thomas and Beulah Hord. The first half of the book is subtitled "Mandolin." It consists of twenty-three poems about Thomas. The second half, "Canary in Bloom," is made up of twenty-one poems about Beulah. The two sets of poems are interwoven. Thomas and Beulah sometimes tell the same stories in

their poems. But they emphasize different parts of their relationship that were more important to each of them.[9]

Thomas and Beulah's lives were simple. Dove explained, "They didn't endure a train wreck or anything like that." However, they faced life's daily challenges in a "quietly heroic way."[10] But even though Thomas and Beulah are of very humble origins, Dove draws the reader into caring for them. She makes her grandparents a compelling couple. She celebrates how they "maintain their goodness despite the struggles they undergo, and pass onto their children the value of dignity and the power of imagination."[11]

Poet Laureate

Dove has written many books in the years that followed *Thomas and Beulah*. She wrote three more poetry collections: *Grace Notes*, *Selected Poems*, and *Mother Love*. She also wrote a novel (*Through the Ivory Gate*) and a collection of short stories (*Fifth Sunday*). She even wrote a verse drama (*The Darker Face of Earth*).

In 1993, she was appointed to a two-year term as poet laureate of the United States. She was the youngest poet to ever earn that distinction. She was also the first African American to be so honored. She said being named "the spokesperson for literature and poetry in this country," made her "an automatic role model." She particularly enjoyed using her position to encourage young people to explore the possibilities of poetry.[12]

The year 1996 was a busy one for Dove. She cohosted a gathering of Nobel laureates in Literature, along with former President Jimmy Carter. The meeting was held in connection with the 1996 Olympic Games in Atlanta. She also wrote the text for a symphonic work by Alvin Singleton commissioned for the Atlanta Olympics. It was

called *Umoja—Each One of Us Counts*. Dove's poem was recited by a narrator in the middle of a symphonic work played by an orchestra.[13]

Dove has provided text for major musical works by composers Tania Leon, Bruce Adolphe, and John Williams (of Boston Symphony Orchestra fame). Dove has served the muse of poetry through membership in a variety of organizations, among them the American Academy of Arts and Sciences, the American Philosophical Society, the National Advisory Board on Student Achievement and Advocacy Services, the National Endowment for the Arts poetry panel, and the Pulitzer Prize jury in poetry. She has also served on the advisory boards of key literary publications, including *Ploughshares*, *Callaloo*, the *Gettysburg Review*, the *Mid-America Review*, and the *Georgia Review*.

In addition to her Pulitzer Prize, Dove has been the recipient of the Portia Pittman Fellowship for Humanities Writer-in-Residence, a Guggenheim grant, a National Humanities Medal, the Virginia Commonwealth Award for Distinguished Service, a General Electric Foundation Award, the Library of Virginia Lifetime Achievement Award, plus more than twenty honorary degrees.

Lifting Up the Downtrodden

Unlike the poets from the black arts movement who came before her, Dove usually writes in more traditional poetic styles. She sometimes writes in free verse. But she enjoys the challenges of "playing around" with "well-made boxes,"[14] and writing in more defined patterns of rhyme and rhythm. She doesn't limit herself to writing about the African-American experience. But she often celebrates the dignity of lowly people in her poems.

Rita Dove

First lady Hillary Rodham Clinton, flanked by poet laureates Robert Pinsky (1997–2000) and Rita Dove (1993–1995), gives a thumbs-up during a Poetry Slam competition at Johnson High School in Washington, D.C., April 22, 1998.

In her Pulitzer Prize–winning collection *Thomas and Beulah*, she tells the story of two poor, young people struggling to get by. She starts by introducing Thomas and his friend Lem in the poem "The Event":

> *Ever since they'd left the Tennessee ridge*
> *with nothing to boast of*
> *but good looks and a mandolin,*
> *the two Negroes leaning*
> *on the rail of a riverboat*
> *were inseparable...*[15]

After telling the story of her grandparents' lives through the eyes of Thomas, Dove reexamines it from her grandmother's point of view. The opening lines of the poem "Weathering Out" describe a typical morning in the life of a very-pregnant Beulah:

> *She liked the mornings the best—Thomas gone*
> *to look for work, her coffee flushed with milk,*
>
> *outside autumn trees blowsy and dripping.*
> *Past the seventh month she couldn't see her feet*
>
> *so she floated from room to room, houseshoes flapping,*
> *navigating corners in wonder...*[16]

Whether or not Dove uses a "formal" writing style in her poems, she tries to bring a sense of musicality to her work.[17] Her lyric *Umoja—Each One of Us Counts* celebrates the 100th anniversary of the modern Olympic Games. *Umoja* pays tribute to the people who are not victorious:

> *Let us honor the lost, the snatched, the relinquished,*
> *those vanquished by glory, muted by shame.*
> *Stand up in the silence they've left and listen:*
> *those absent ones, unknown and unnamed—*
>
> *remember!*
> *their whispers fill the arena.*[18]

Today, Dove is the Commonwealth Professor of English at the University of Virginia in Charlottesville. She continues to write poems and to pursue her interest in music. She has written texts for several classical-style songs. She also takes opera lessons and plays the viola de gamba, a 17th-century predecessor of the modern cello.[19]

Dove's writing draws from a number of different experiences. It does not readily fit into any single category. As she herself once admitted, "I'm an African-American poet; I'm a woman poet; I'm an American poet; all those things. But I'm a poet first."[20]

Rita Dove Timeline

1952—Rita Dove is born on August 28 in Akron, Ohio.

1970—Dove is named a Presidential Scholar.

1973—Graduates summa cum laude from Miami University in Oxford, Ohio.

1977—Receives her MFA in creative writing and publishes a chapbook of poetry.

1980— *The Yellow House on the Corner*, a collection of poetry, is published.

1983—*Museum*, a collection of poetry, is published.

1985—*Fifth Sunday*, a collection of short stories, is published.

1986—*Thomas and Beulah* is published; it wins a Pulitzer Prize in 1987.

1988—*The Other Side of the House*, a book of poetry, is published.

1989—*Grace Notes*, a book of poetry, is published.

1992—*Through the Ivory Gate*, a novel, is published.

1993—Dove is the youngest person and first African American to be appointed poet laureate of the United States.

1994—*The Darker Face of the Earth*, a verse play, is published.

Timeline

1995—*Mother Love*, a book of poetry, and *The Poet's World*, a book of essays, are published.

1999—*On the Bus With Rosa Parks*, a book of poetry, is published.

2004—*American Smooth*, a book of poetry, is published.

2006—Dove is elected a chancellor of the Academy of American Poets.

2009—*Sonata Mulattica*, a book of poetry, is published.

Chapter Notes

Introduction

1. Michael Harper and Anthony Walton, eds., *The Vintage Book of African American Poetry* (New York: Random House, 2000), p. xxv.
2. Ibid.
3. Ibid, p. 21.
4. Henry Louis Gates, Jr., and Nellie Y. McKay, eds., *The Norton Anthology of African American Literature* (New York: Norton, 1997), pp. xxviii–xxix.
5. Harper and Walton, p. xxvi.
6. Ibid.
7. Ibid., pp. 113–114.
8. Ibid., p. xxviii.
9. Gates and McKay, p. 2582.
10. Ibid., p. xxxiii.
11. Ibid., p. xxviii.

Chapter 1
Phillis Wheatley

1. "Phillis Wheatley: America's First Black Woman Poet," *Archiving Early America*, n.d. <http://www .earlyamerica.com/review/winter96/wheatley .htm> (June 2, 2008).
2. "Women in History. Phillis Wheatley Biography," *Lakewood Public Library*, n.d. <http://www.lkwdpl .org/wihohio/whea-phi.htm> (June 2, 2008).
3. "Memoir and Poems of Phillis Wheatley, a Native African and a Slave," *Documenting the American South*, n.d <http://docsouth.unc.edu/neh/wheatley/ wheatley.html> (June 2, 2008).
4. Ibid.
5. Ibid.

6. "Phillis Wheatley (1753–1784)," *PAL: Perspectives in American Literature—A Research and Reference Guide*, n.d. <http://web. csustan.edu/english/reuben/pal/chap2/wheatley. html> (June 2, 2008).

7. Ibid.

8. Phillis Wheatley, "On Being Brought from Africa to America," *The Norton Anthology of African American Literature*, ed. Henry Louis Gates, Jr., and Nellie Y. McKay (New York: Norton, 1997), p. 171.

9. Phillis Wheatley, "To the Right Honourable William, Earl of Dartmouth, His Majesty's Principal Secretary of State for North-America, Etc.," *The Norton Anthology of African American Literature*, ed. Henry Louis Gates, Jr., and Nellie Y. McKay (New York: Norton, 1997), p. 173.

10. "Memoir and Poems of Phillis Wheatley, a Native African and a Slave," *Documenting the American South*, n.d. <http://docsouth.unc.edu/neh/wheatley/wheatley.html> (June 2, 2008).

11. Ibid.

12. David Lander, "The Prodigy," *American Legacy*, Summer 2002, p. 74.

13. "Phillis Wheatley (1753–1784)," *PAL: Perspectives in American Literature—A Research and Reference Guide*, n.d. <http://web. csustan.edu/english/reuben/pal/chap2/wheatley. html> (June 2, 2008).

14. "Memoir and Poems of Phillis Wheatley, a Native African and a Slave," *Documenting the American South*, n.d. <http://docsouth.unc.edu/neh/wheatley/wheatley.html> (June 2, 2008).

15. "Phillis Wheatley (1753–1784)," *PAL: Perspectives in American Literature—A Research and Reference Guide*, n.d. <http://web. csustan.edu/english/reuben/pal/chap2/wheatley. html> (June 2, 2008).

16. Lander, p. 74.

17. "Memoir and Poems of Phillis Wheatley, a Native African and a Slave," *Documenting the American South*, n.d. <http://docsouth.unc.edu/neh/wheatley/wheatley.html> (June 2, 2008).

18. Michael Harper and Anthony Walton, eds., *The Vintage Book of African American Poetry* (New York: Random House, 2000), p. 13.

19. Henry Louis Gates, Jr., and Nellie Y. McKay, eds., *The Norton Anthology of African American Literature* (New York: Norton, 1997), p. xxxiii.

20. Erin Aubry Kaplan, "Remade in America," *Los Angeles Times Book Review*, December 23, 2007, p. R8.

Chapter 2
Paul Laurence Dunbar

1. "The Paul Laurence Dunbar Website," *The University of Dayton*, n.d. <http://www.dunbarsite.org/biopld.asp.> (June 2, 2008).

2. Henry Louis Gates, Jr., and Nellie Y. McKay, eds., *The Norton Anthology of African American Literature* (New York: Norton, 1997), p. 884.

3. "The Paul Laurence Dunbar Website," *The University of Dayton*, n.d. <http://www.dunbarsite.org/biopld.asp> (June 2, 2008).

4. Ibid.

5. Gates and McKay, p. 885.

6. "The Paul Laurence Dunbar Website," *The University of Dayton*, n.d. <http://www.dunbarsite.org/biopld.asp> (June 2, 2008).

7. Ibid.

8. Ibid.

94

9. Michael Harper and Anthony Walton, eds., *The Vintage Book of African American Poetry* (New York: Random House, 2000), p. 72.

10. "The Paul Laurence Dunbar Website," *The University of Dayton*, n.d. <http://www.dunbarsite .org/biopld.asp> (June 2, 2008).

11. Gates and McKay, p. 886.

12. "Paul Dunbar: Our Own History Books," *Dayton History Books Online*, n.d. <http://www .daytonhistorybooks.com/halloffamedunbar.html> (June 2, 2008).

13. Gates and McKay, p. 886.

14. Harper and Walton, p. 72.

15. Paul Laurence Dunbar, "When Malindy Sings," *The Vintage Book of African American Poetry*, ed. Michael Harper and Anthony Walton (New York: Random House, 2000), p. 75.

16. Ibid., p. 72.

17. Ibid.

18. Paul Laurence Dunbar, "We Wear the Mask," *The Vintage Book of African American Poetry*, ed. Michael Harper and Anthony Walton (New York: Random House, 2000), p. 76.

19. Paul Laurence Dunbar, "Sympathy," *The Vintage Book of African American Poetry*, ed. Michael Harper and Anthony Walton (New York: Random House, 2000), p. 77.

20. Ibid., p. 72.

21. "The Paul Laurence Dunbar Website," *The University of Dayton*, n.d. <http://www.dunbarsite.org/biopld. asp> (June 2, 2008).

22. "Dunbar House," *The Ohio Historical Society* <http:// ohsweb.ohiohistory.org/places/sw03/> (June 2, 2008).

Chapter 3
Langston Hughes

1. Henry Louis Gates, Jr., and Nellie Y. McKay, eds., *The Norton Anthology of African American Literature* (New York: Norton, 1997), pp. 1251–1252.

2. "Langston Hughes in Kansas," *Kansas History: A Journal of the Central Plains*, 1980 Index, *Kansas State Historical Society*, n.d. <http://www.kshs.org/publicat/history/1980spring_scott.pdf> (June 4, 2008).

3. Ibid.

4. Arnold Rampersad and David Roessel, eds., *The Collected Poems of Langston Hughes* (New York: Knopf, 1996), p. 8.

5. Gates and McKay, p. 1252.

6. Rampersad and Roessel, pp. 9–10.

7. "Langston Hughes in Kansas," *Kansas History: A Journal of the Central Plains*, 1980 Index, *Kansas State Historical Society*, n.d. <http://www.kshs.org/publicat/history/1980spring_scott.pdf> (June 4, 2008).

8. Langston Hughes, "The Negro Artist and the Racial Mountain," *The Norton Anthology of African American Literature*, ed. Henry Louis Gates, Jr., and Nellie Y. McKay (New York: Norton, 1997), p. 1267.

9. Rampersad and Roessel, p. 9.

10. Gates and McKay, p. 1251.

11. Langston Hughes, "Harlem," *The Norton Anthology of African American Literature*, ed. Henry Louis Gates, Jr., and Nellie Y. McKay (New York: Norton, 1997), p. 1267.

12. Langston Hughes, "The Weary Blues," *The Norton Anthology of African American Literature*, ed. Henry

Louis Gates, Jr., and Nellie Y. McKay (New York: Norton, 1997), p. 1257.

13. Langston Hughes, "Mother to Son," *The Norton Anthology of African American Literature*, ed. Henry Louis Gates, Jr., and Nellie Y. McKay (New York: Norton, 1997), p. 1255.

14. "Langston Hughes in Kansas," *Kansas History: A Journal of the Central Plains*, 1980 Index, *Kansas State Historical Society*, n.d. <http://www.kshs.org/publicat/history/1980spring_scott.pdf> (June 4, 2008).

15. Gates and McKay, p. 1254.

Chapter 4
Gwendolyn Brooks

1. "Gwendolyn Brooks," *Gale Cengage Learning*, n.d. <http://www.gale.cengage.com/free_resources/bhm/bio/brooks_g.html.> (June 6, 2008).

2. "Gwendolyn Brooks," *Illinois Poet Laureate*, n.d. <http://www2.illinois.gov/poetlaureate/Pages/brooks.aspx> (June 6, 2008).

3. "Gwendolyn Brooks," *Gale Cengage Learning*, n.d. <http://www.gale.cengage.com/free_resources/bhm/bio/brooks_g.html> (June 6, 2008).

4. "Gwendolyn Brooks," *Illinois Poet Laureate*, n.d. <http://www2.illinois.gov/poetlaureate/Pages/brooks.aspx> (June 6, 2008).

5. "Brooks' Life and Career," *Modern American Poetry*, n.d. <http://www.english.illinois.edu/maps/poets/a_f/brooks/life.html> (June 6, 2008).

6. "Gwendolyn Brooks," *Gale Cengage Learning*, n.d. <http://www.gale.cengage.com/free_resources/bhm/bio/brooks_g.html> (June 6, 2008).

7. Ibid.

8. Ibid.

9. Gwendolyn Brooks, "The Rites for Cousin Vit," *The Norton Anthology of African American Literature*, ed. Henry Louis Gates, Jr., and Nellie Y. McKay (New York: Norton, 1997), p. 1586.

10. Gwendolyn Brooks, "We Real Cool," *The Norton Anthology of African American Literature*, ed. Henry Louis Gates, Jr., and Nellie Y. McKay (New York: Norton, 1997), p. 1591.

11. "Gwendolyn Brooks," Gale Cengage Learning, n.d. <http://www.gale.cengage.com/free_resources/bhm/bio/brooks_g.html> (June 6, 2008).

12. "Gwendolyn Brooks," *Illinois Poet Laureate*, n.d. <http://www2.illinois.gov/poetlaureate/Pages/brooks.aspx> (June 6, 2008).

13. "Testifying–A Tribute by Rita Dove," *James Madison University*, n.d. <http://www.jmu.edu/furiousflower/dove_tribute_brooks.shtml> (November 3, 2008).

Chapter 5
Amiri Baraka

1. "Amiri Baraka (LeRoi Jones): The Man, the Poet, and the Myth," *Poetry Previews*, n.d. <http://www.poetrypreviews.com/poets/poet-baraka.html> (June 12, 2008).

2. "Amiri Baraka," *Books and Writers*, n.d. <http://www.kirjasto.sci.fi/Baraka/htm> (June 12, 2008).

3. Henry Louis Gates, Jr., and Nellie Y. McKay, eds., *The Norton Anthology of African American Literature* (New York: Norton, 1997), p. 1877.

4. "Amiri Baraka (LeRoi Jones): The Man, the Poet, and the Myth," *Poetry Previews*, n.d <http://www.poetrypreviews.com/poets/poet-baraka.html> (June 12, 2008).

5. "Amiri Baraka," *The African American Registry*, n.d. <http://www.aaregistry.com/historic_events/view/amiri-baraka-controversial-poet-and-playwright> (June 15, 2008).

6. Ibid.

7. Gates and McKay, p. 1878.

8. "Amiri Baraka," *Books and Writers*, n.d. <http://www.kirjasto.sci.fi/Baraka.htm> (June 12, 2008).

9. Ibid.

10. Gates and McKay, p. 1878.

11. "Amiri Baraka (LeRoi Jones): The Man, the Poet, and the Myth," *Poetry Previews*, n.d <http://www.poetrypreviews.com/poets/poet-baraka.html> (June 12, 2008).

12. Gates and McKay, p. 1878.

13. Ibid.

14. "Amiri Baraka," *The African American Registry*, n.d <http://www.aaregistry.com/historic_events/view/amiri-baraka-controversial-poet-and-playwright> (June 15, 2008).

15. "Amiri Baraka (LeRoi Jones): The Man, the Poet, and the Myth," *Poetry Previews*, n.d. <http://www.poetrypreviews.com/poets/poet-baraka.html> (June 12, 2008).

16. Ibid.

17. Amiri Baraka, "Foreword," *Black Fire: An Anthology of Afro-American Writing* (New York: Apollo Editions, 1969), p. xvii.

18. Willis Wager, "Poetry," *Living History of the World: 1971 Yearbook* (New York: Stavon Educational Press, 1971), p. 324.

19. Amiri Baraka, "Return of the Native," *Children of Promise: African-American Literature and Art for Young People* (New York: Harry N. Abrams, 1991), p. 88.

20. Amiri Baraka, "Poem for Black Hearts," *I Am the Darker Brother: An Anthology of Modern Poems by African Americans* (New York: Simon and Schuster, 1997), pp. 87–88.

21. Amiri Baraka, "Young Soul," *Children of Promise: African-American Literature and Art for Young People* (New York: Harry N. Abrams, 1991), p. 11.

22. Amiri Baraka Biography, n.d. <http://www .amiribaraka.com> (June 12, 2008).

23. "Amiri Baraka," *Books and Writers*, n.d. <http:// www.kirjasto.sci.fi/Baraka.htm> (June 12, 2008).

24. Ibid.

25. Ibid.

Chapter 6
Jay Wright

1. "Jay Wright," *Poetry Foundation*, n.d. <http:// www.poetryfoundation.org/bio/jay-wright> (June 10, 2008).

2. "Book Review: Transfigurations," *Boston Review: A Political and Literary Forum*, n.d. <http:// bostonreview .net/BR27.2/meyer.html> (June 10, 2008).

3. Jay Wright, "Introduction to Play Ebony, Play Ivory," *Chicken Bones: A Journal for Literary and Artistic African-American Themes*, n.d. <http://

nathanielturner.com/introplayebony.htm>
(November 4, 2008).

4. "Jay Wright," *Poetry Foundation*, n.d. <http://
www
.poetryfoundation.org/bio/jay-wright> (June 10,
2008).

5. Ibid.

6. Ibid.

7. "Book Review: Transfigurations," *Boston Review:
A Political and Literary Forum*, n.d. <http://
bostonreview.net/BR27.2/meyer.html> (June 10,
2008).

8. Jay Wright, "The Albuquerque Graveyard," *The
Vintage Book of African American Poetry*, Michael
S. Harper and Anthony Walton, eds. (New York:
Random House, 2000), p. 257.

9. Jay Wright, "Meta-A and the A of Absolutes," *The
Vintage Book of African American Poetry*, Michael
S. Harper and Anthony Walton, eds. (New York:
Random House, 2000), p. 259.

10. "Poet, Essayist and Playwright Jay Wright to
Read for UA Poetry Center," *University of Arizona
Office of Communications*, n.d. <http://uanews.org/
node/6075> (June 10, 2008).

11. Jay Wright, "The Healing Improvisation of Hair,"
The Vintage Book of African American Poetry, Michael
S. Harper and Anthony Walton, eds. (New York:
Random House, 2000), p. 256.

Chapter 7
Nikki Giovanni

1. Kathy Y. Wilson, "Saying it Loud," *Cincinnati
Magazine*, April 2008, p. 114.

2. "Nikki Giovanni," *Ohioana Authors*, n.d. <http://www.ohioana-authors.org/giovanni/highlights.php> (June 18, 2008).

3. Wilson, p. 150.

4. "Nikki Giovanni," *Ohioana Authors*, n.d. <http://www.ohioana-authors.org/giovanni/highlights.php> (June 18, 2008).

5. Wilson, p. 114.

6. Ibid., p. 112.

7. "Nikki Giovanni," *Ohioana Authors*, n.d. <http://www.ohioana-authors.org/giovanni/highlights.php> (June 18, 2008).

8. Wilson, p. 151.

9. Ibid., p. 115.

10. Nikki Giovanni, "The Funeral of Dr. Martin Luther King, Jr.," *Children of Promise: African-American Literature and Art for Young People* (New York: Harry N. Abrams, 1991), p. 106.

11. "Nikki Giovanni," *Ohioana Authors*, n.d. <http://www.ohioana-authors.org/giovanni/highlights.php> (June 18, 2008).

12. Nikki Giovanni, "Nikki-Rosa," *I Am the Darker Brother: An Anthology of Modern Poems by African Americans* (New York: Simon and Schuster, 1997), p. 29.

13. "Nikki Giovanni," *Ohioana Authors*, n.d. <http://www.ohioana-authors.org/giovanni/highlights.php> (June 18, 2008).

14. "Biography," *Nikki Giovanni*, n.d. <http://nikki-giovanni.com/bio.shtml> (June 18, 2008).

15. Wilson, p. 115.

Chapter 8
Rita Dove

1. "An Interview With Rita Dove by M. W. Thomas: August 12, 1995," *Modern American Poetry*, n.d. <http://www.english.uiuc.edu/maps/poets/a_f/dove/mwthomas.htm> (November 4, 2008).

2. "Rita Dove," *Women of Color, Women of Words*, n.d. <http://www.scils.rutgers.edu/~cybers/dove.html> (June 19, 2008).

3. Thomas.

4. Ibid.

5. Ibid.

6. Ibid.

7. Ibid.

8. Ibid.

9. Henry Louis Gates, Jr., and Nellie Y. McKay, eds., *The Norton Anthology of African American Literature* (New York: Norton, 1997), p. 2583.

10. "An Interview With Rita Dove by M. W. Thomas: August 12, 1995," *Modern American Poetry*, n.d. <http://www.english.uiuc.edu/maps/poets/a_f/dove/mwthomas.htm> (November 4, 2008).

11. Gates and McKay, p. 2583.

12. "Rita Dove," *Academy of Achievement*, n.d. <http://www.achievement.org/autodoc/page/dove0bio-1> (June 19, 2008).

13. "An Interview With Rita Dove by M. W. Thomas: August 12, 1995," *Modern American Poetry*, n.d. <http://www.english.uiuc.edu/maps/poets/a_f/dove/mwthomas.htm> (November 4, 2008).

14. Ibid.

15. Rita Dove, "The Event," *The Vintage Book of African American Poetry*, Michael Harper and Anthony Walton, eds. (New York: Random House, 2000), p. 349.
16. Rita Dove, "Weathering Out," *The Vintage Book of African American Poetry*, Michael Harper and Anthony Walton, eds. (New York: Random House, 2000), p. 350.
17. "An Online Interview With Rita Dove: June 18, 1994," *Modern American Poetry*, n.d. <http://www.english.uiuc.edu/maps/poets/a_f/dove/onlineinterviews.htm> (June 19, 2008).
18. Rita Dove, "Umoja—Each One of Us Counts," *The Nation*, n.d. <http://www.thenation.com/article/poets-against-war> (November 4, 2008).
19. "Rita Dove," *Academy of Achievement*, n.d. <http://www.achievement.org/autodoc/page/dove0bio-1> (June 19, 2008).
20. "An Online Interview With Rita Dove: June 18, 1994," *Modern American Poetry*,n.d. <http://www.english.uiuc.edu/maps/poets/a_f/dove/onlineinterviews.htm> (June 19, 2008).

Glossary

American Civil War—The war between the northern and southern United States that occurred between 1861 and 1865.

Beat movement—A period featuring a group of American poets and novelists of the 1950s and 1960s—including Jack Kerouac, Allen Ginsberg, William S. Burroughs, and Lawrence Ferlinghetti—who rejected established social and literary values.

blues—Music about life's troubles and sorrows.

civil war—A war between groups of citizens of the same country.

free verse—Poetic lines composed without a set rhyme scheme or meter.

Great Depression—A period of approximately ten years, starting in 1929, when many banks, factories, and stores went out of business. Millions of people lost their jobs and sometimes their homes too.

Harlem Renaissance—The Harlem Renaissance of the 1920s is generally considered the first significant movement of poets, writers, and artists in the United States. During this period, new and established black writers published more fiction and poetry than ever before along with the first widespread recognition and serious critical appraisal.

imagery—Figurative language.

jazz—Music with a strong rhythm, used to show feelings and ideas. Jazz is mainly performed with instruments, and the musicians often make up new parts as they play the music.

poem—A composition using rhyme, meter, concrete detail, and expressive language to create a literary experience with emotional and aesthetic appeal.

poet laureate—A recognized eminent poet appointed to promote poetry and to represent a country or locality.

Revolutionary War—The war between Great Britain and the thirteen American colonies that was fought from 1775 to 1783. It resulted in the Americans' setting up a free and independent country.

rhyme—Arrangement of words by the final sound or sounds; lines of poetry may rhyme within the line or more usually at its end with another line.

 rhythm—A regular pattern of sound, time intervals, or events occurring in writing, most often and most discernibly in poetry.

scholarship—Money that is given to a student to help pay for his or her studies.

slang—A type of informal verbal communication that is generally unacceptable for formal writing.

sonnet—A poem with fourteen lines of iambic pentameter verse, with a variety of rhyme patterns, based on an Italian form made popular by Petrarch.

stanza—A verse or set of lines grouped together and set apart from the rest of the poem, like a paragraph in prose writing.

symbolism—A late-nineteenth-century movement in French art and literature in which objects have symbolic meaning.

theme—The main point of a work of literature.

verse—A line of metered language, a line of a poem, or any work in verse.

World War II—A war fought from 1939 to 1945. The United States, Great Britain, the Soviet Union, and their allies were on one side; Germany, Italy, Japan, and their allies were on the other.

Further Reading

Adoff, Arnold. *I Am the Darker Brother: An Anthology of Modern Poems by African Americans*. New York: Simon Pulse, 1997.

Bloom, Harold, ed. *Gwendolyn Brooks*. Philadelphia: Chelsea House Publishers, 2005.

Brooks, Gwendolyn. *Bronzeville Boys and Girls*. New York: Amistad, 2006.

Clinton, Catherine. *I, Too, Sing America: Three Centuries of African American Poetry*. New York: Houghton Mifflin, 1998.

Giovanni, Nikki. *Hip Hop Speaks to Children: A Celebration of Poetry With a Beat*. New York: Sourcebooks Jabberwocky; Har/Com edition, 2008.

Rampersad, Arnold and David Roessel, eds. *Poetry for Young People: Langston Hughes*. New York: Sterling, 2006.

Rochelle, Belinda. *Words With Wings: A Treasury of African-American Poetry and Art*. New York: Amistad, 2000.

Wallace, Maurice. *Langston Hughes: The Harlem Renaissance*. New York: Marshall Cavendish Benchmark, 2008.

African American Poets—Famous Black Poets

Includes biographies and sample poems by dozens of African Americans who have written poetry over the past 250 years.

<http://famouspoetsandpoems.com/poets_african_american.html>

Poets.Org—From the Academy of American Poets

Permissions

Jay Wright

"The Albuquerque Graveyard," first published in *Soothsayers and Omens* (Seven Woods Press, 1976), copyright © Jay Wright. Reprinted in *Transfigurations: Collected Poems* (Louisiana State University Press, 2000), copyright © Jay Wright. Reprinted by permission of the author.

"Meta-A and the A of Absolutes," first published in *Dimensions of History* (Kayak Books, 1976), copyright © Jay Wright. Reprinted in *Transfigurations: Collected Poems* (Louisiana State University Press, 2000), Copyright © Jay Wright. Reprinted by permission of the author.

"The Healing Improvisation of Hair," from *Transformations*. Reprinted in *Transfigurations: Collected Poems* (Louisiana State University Press, 2000), copyright © Jay Wright. Reprinted by permission of the author.

Langston Hughes

"Harlem (2) ["What happens to a dream deferred…"]", "Mother to Son," "The Weary Blues" from THE COLLECTED POEMS OF LANGSTON HUGHES by Langston Hughes, edited by Arnold Rampersad with David Roessel, Associate Editor, copyright © 1994 by the Estate of Langston Hughes. Used by permission of Alfred A. Knopf, a division of Random House, Inc.

Nikki Giovanni

"The Funeral of Dr. Martin Luther King, Jr." COPYRIGHT © 1968, 1970 BY NIKKI GIOVANNI. Reprinted by permission of HarperCollins Publishers.

"Nikki Rosa." COPYRIGHT © 1968, 1970 BY NIKKI GIOVANNI. Reprinted by permission of HarperCollins Publishers.

"Virginia Tech." COPYRIGHT © 2009 BY NIKKI GIOVANNI. Reprinted by permission of HarperCollins Publishers.

Rita Dove

"The Event" and "Weathering Out" in *Thomas and Beulah*, Carnegie-Mellon University Press, Pittsburgh, PA. Copyright © 1986 by Rita Dove. Reprinted by permission of the author.

"Umoja—Each One of Us Counts" was originally written for the Atlanta Olympic Games as part of a symphonic work with music by Alvin Singleton first performed at Atlanta Symphony Hall during the Olympic Games' opening weekend in the summer of 1996 (read by former Atlanta mayor and United States ambassador to the United Nations Andrew Young). The concert was broadcast on National Public Radio, and the poem was printed in the live concert's program notes. Subsequently, it was printed as a stand-alone poem in "Poets Against the War," *The Nation*, March 10, 2003. Copyright © 1996 by Rita Dove. Reprinted by permission of the author.

Index